Demonology as Devourment Without a Devourer

The Movies of Keanu Reeves and Other Ways to Study Demons

CollectiveInk

First published by Sixth Books, 2026
Sixth Books is an imprint of Collective Ink Ltd.,
Unit 11, Shepperton House, 89 Shepperton Road, London, N1 3DF
office@collectiveinkbooks.com
www.collectiveinkbooks.com
www.6th-books.com

For distributor details and how to order please visit the 'Ordering' section on our website.

ISBN: 978 1 917704 03 8
978 1 917704 35 9 (ebook)
Library of Congress Control Number: 2025905142

A CIP catalogue record for this book is available from the British Library.

Design: Lapiz Digital Services

UK: Printed and bound by CPI Group (UK) Ltd, Croydon, CR0 4YY
Printed in North America by CPI GPS partners

The manufacturer's authorised representative in the EU for product safety is: eucomply OÜ - Pärnu mnt 139b-14, 11317 Tallinn, Estonia, hello@ eucompliancepartner.com, www.eucompliancepartner.com

Praise for *Demonology as Devourment Without a Devourer*

Ben-Yosef's secular demonology cuts to the root of human self-negation, casting urgent light on why so many of us feel devoured by forces we scarcely acknowledge—and how to break free. An indispensable guide for anyone bold enough to face the future head-on.

Jason Louv, bestselling author of *John Dee and the Empire of Angels* and host of the *Ultraculture with Jason Louv* podcast

Demonology as Devourment Without a Devourer

The Movies of Keanu Reeves and Other Ways to Study Demons

Oren Ben-Yosef

6TH BOOKS

London, UK
Washington, DC, USA

Thank you:

To the people of 6th Books, for believing in this work.
To Idan Margalit, for the ongoing, intense and provocative discussions on things that should be spoken of and things that shouldn't.
To Klaudia Doppelt, for correcting my English.
To my family, for bearing with all of this.
To my wife, Ori, an angel among demons, for pushing me when I'm getting tired of flying and for everything else in my life.

Table of Contents

Introduction: Heresy and Horror

> Life is a hideous thing, and from the background behind what we know of it peer daemoniacal hints of truth which makes it sometimes a thousandfold more hideous. Science, already oppressive with its shocking revelations, will perhaps be the ultimate exterminator of our human species — if separate species we be — for its reserve of unguessed horrors could never be borne by mortal brains if loosed upon the world. If we knew what we are, we should do as Sir Arthur Jermyn did; and Arthur Jermyn soaked himself in oil and set fire to his clothing one night.
>
> H. P. Lovecraft, *Facts concerning the Late Arthur Jermyn and His Family*.[1]

Right before the climax of the movie *The Devil's Advocate* (Hackford, 1997), successful and immoral lawyer, Kevin Lomax, is walking on his way to his last conversation with his mysterious boss, John Milton. In this long-shot walking scene, viewers who have not already sensed that Milton, named after the author of the epic poem *Paradise Lost*, is much more than a mere human, should realize that Lomax is no longer walking in our own reality. The streets of New York are utterly empty — an unbelievable scene to be imagined in a pre-Covid New York. Watching this scene, I couldn't help but think about author Nick Land's opening for the first chapter in his book *The Thirst for Annihilation*, in which Land writes that to be transcendental is to be "free" of reality.[2] Lomax is not free from the binding of reality, but he is indeed suspended from it before his final conversation with Milton, who is revealed to be twice horrific. He is Lomax's father. He is also the devil.

But Milton does indeed offer Lomax freedom from reality. Not transcendent in any way, Lomax will enjoy a successful life of every temptation fulfilled and all shame and guilt eradicated. Lomax's mother is a devout Christian, reminding him and us of the hierarchy of light above darkness, of servitude above the succumbing to sin, while his father demands the exact opposite. In his speech, Milton describes God as a sadist ruler who forces impossible conditions on mankind. God created man with specific, hard-wired instincts and passions, only to then order him to ignore them and live a life strictly opposed to these basic human characteristics. Milton (Satan) is a humanist, or so he declares. He wants mankind to live the way mankind wants to live. Instead of blind servitude to a hidden God, Milton offers free will.

In this scene, Satan offers a different reading to the Bible and to God in general. Such subversive readings are at the foundation of all heresy, as heresy is not only the act of defying the strict rule of God, but also the act of telling a different angle of his story. In Jorges Luis Borges' story, *Three Versions of Judas*,[3] a heresy not smaller in magnitude is being told, even though it does not challenge God's divine rule over the Earth. This is a story about fictitious writer Nils Runeberg, who offers a different reading to the story of Judas' betrayal of Jesus. The first version of his story suggests that Judas was a mere reflection of Jesus in the world of man, accepting sin upon himself in order to elevate the son of God. His second version suggested that among the two of them, it was actually Judas who sacrificed the most, as while Jesus was degraded in body, Judas was degraded in spirit. Runeberg's third, most heretic suggestion, is that God, in human shape, would have to be entirely human, meaning a sinner. In this version, Runeberg suggests that the son of God was actually Judas and not Jesus. Another notorious heresy, not fictional but theological, is of course the heresy of philosopher Spinoza, who suggested an immanent, pantheistic God, rather than a transcendent one.

This book opens with the climax of *The Devil's Advocate*, not because it deals with heresy in a strict way, nor because it deals directly with the devil. It opens with this movie because the following chapters will suggest a reading of Demonology, while analysing several other movies that have a specific thing in common with *The Devil's Advocate*, and that is that their protagonists are all played by actor Keanu Reeves. While this experimental reading of the movies is not meant to say anything about the actor himself (except the fact that I like his movies), it does offer an otherwise unlikely connection between the worlds of these movies — a connection that I hope will be in my favor in discussing Demonology in a contemporary, secular way.

This book does not discuss the existence of demons in any Judeo-Christian meaning, and as I will explain in this introduction, as well as in the following chapters, it has little to nothing to do with Satan or satanism. Indeed, while *The Devil's Advocate* offers a story about the Anti-Christian opposition to Judeo-Christianity, a contemporary, secular Demonology discusses something else in its entirety — the negation of man into an uncaring nothingness and the abolition of the human's sovereignty over himself. In other words, this is not a warning against, or even discussion about damnation by the hands of the adversary, but about the possibility of annihilation by the hands of an uncaring non-humanity.

We see this, I will argue, in three movies or series of movies, all starring Keanu Reeves, and these movies are the movie *Constantine* (Lawrence, 2005), *John Wick 1–4* (Stahelski, 2014, 2017, 2019, 2023) and *The Matrix 1–3* (The Wachowskis, 1999, 2003, 2003). Hints for these movies can be found by the end of *The Devil's Advocate*. When Lomax is walking down an empty boulevard, one cannot help but think about the gradual disappearance of humans in all of these movies, to be discussed later on. When John Milton tells Lomax that he intends to take over the world by taking over the system of laws and justice, one cannot help but think about the system of laws between heaven and hell in *Constantine,* the all-encompassing system of laws and bureaucracy in the movies of *John Wick* and the Gnosis that allows the bending of physical rules in *The Matrix*. Ultimately, Lomax's encounter with Satan results in the suicide of the protagonist, an action that initiates John Constantine's final dialogue with the same ruler of hell.

But the ending of *The Devil's Advocate,* in which Lomax discovers, much to his horror, that he is the son of Satan, brings to mind another story, this time by the master of cosmic horror, H. P. Lovecraft. In this story, *Facts concerning the Late Arthur Jermyn and His Family,* Arthur Jermyn also discover that he is in fact a descendant of a horrific ape-goddess, rather than a normal human being — a discovery that leads him to commit suicide as well. However, there is an important difference between Lovecraft's story and that of *The Devil's Advocate,* being that while Lomax discovers that he is an important pawn in the well-known mythical war between God and Satan, Jermyn discovers that within him there is an essence that is alien, inhuman and unknown. While Lomax is being promised the vast riches resulting from the turning of the godly hierarchy upside down, the only thing promised to Jermyn is the horror of the unknown and the dissolution of anything he knew about himself. The devil cares about mankind. He works hard to corrupt and to dismantle any grip that God might have on humans. The monstrosities in the numerous worlds of Lovecraft are horrific precisely because they are completely ignorant of mankind and of mankind's will, while being hostile and anti-humanist. This is a good starting point of understanding demonology without its religious context.

In this book, I attempt to not portray the idea of demons in the somewhat caricatured method of evil — as intelligent servants of the devil. Rather, old ideas of demonology are brought together with more recent approaches to technology and to ideas of entities as neither living nor supernatural intelligent creatures, but *things* that exist as distinct and independent units. The world is teeming with entities, besides all living things. A city is an entity, as is a tree, a stone and perhaps, although at this level the lines might become blurry — an atom. This book is an entity, like the laptop on which I am writing it right now. What makes demons in their secular definition different from other entities, then, is that these are entities that exist in the world only by the negation of living beings, mankind in particular.

Ultimately, the idea of demonology might conjure thoughts about the deep abyss of the human mind, from which all darkness might erupt. Jungian, Freudian or otherwise, these ideas sit deep inside the human psyche like parasites, leading to a conclusion that may indeed be less dramatic, but still reminiscent of Jermyn's fate — that we are not entirely who we think we are. At this point, while this book at least tries to offer a secular view on Demonology, rather than a mythical ethos, I close this part of the book with an uneasy question to ponder on and to continue my thoughts onwards: is there a possibility that ideas, in some way, preceded mankind and even earlier living creatures, in ways described by St Augustine or Plato, or even different, more alien ways? Indeed, such understanding should qualify as Lovecraft's daemoniacal hints of truth, "which might add more horror to life."

Notes

1. Lovecraft, H. P., Joshi, S. T. (ed.), *The Call of Cthulhu and Other Weird Stories*. London: Penguin Books, 2002, p. 14.
2. Land, Nick, *The Thirst for Annihilation: Georges Bataille and Virulent Nihilism (an Essay in Atheistic Religion)*. London: Routledge, 1992, p. 1.
3. Borges, Jorge Luis, *Collected Fictions*, Andrew Hurley (trans.). London: Penguin Books, 1999, p. 163.

One Being in Three Presences

1.

The Magician Is He Who Can Act in the World – Magus of the Three Worlds

> Therefore, when the word 'magic' is used, it should either be taken in one of the senses distinguished above, or, if it is used without qualifications, it should be taken in its strongest and most worthy sense as dictated by the logicians, and especially by Aristotle in Book V of the *Topics*. So as it is used by and among philosophers, 'magician' then means a wise man who has the power to act.
>
> Giordano Bruno, *On Magic*.[1]

In Neil Gaiman's graphic novel *The Books of Magic,* young Timothy is approached by a group of mysterious individuals who have taken it upon themselves to introduce him to the history and practice of magic. Timothy is then transported to the past, to ancient times when magic used to be a dominant factor in life. He is taken to the land of fairies, where magic is all there is and he is taken to the distant future, when magic finally returns to our world. Timothy, a 12-year-old boy with the still undiscovered potential to become a great magician, is also introduced to a parallel shadow world of magic that exists right next to our everyday, seemingly disenchanted reality. While Timothy's knowledge about the world is somewhat similar to the knowledge other 12-year-old children have, he is introduced to many peculiar characters who live side by side with us, the readers, only these people are different, being magicians, witches and non-human creatures. In this journey to the contemporary occult world, Timothy is accompanied by John Constantine, a notorious occult detective, created by writers Alan Moore and Stephen R. Bissette and most known as the leading character in the *Hellblazer* comic book series.

Constantine introduces Timothy to his friend Zatanna, a witch, who then takes temporary care of the child as Constantine is forced to leave the continent for an urgent mission. Zatanna takes Timothy to a Halloween party, where he meets numerous unsavory characters such as Tala, who is a queen of evil and Tannarak, a sinister black magician. At a certain point, the various wizards, together with the rest of the beings in the party, turn on Timothy in order to catch and even kill the would-be wizard child, disregarding Zatanna's attempts to protect her guest. It is then that Constantine suddenly appears. He lights a cigarette and calmly announces that no one is going to touch Timothy, that he is going to leave together with Zatanna and Timothy, and that no one is going to try and stop them. How could he possibly do that? Zatanna insists on understanding this unsettling mystery. Unlike her, Constantine does not seem to have any power to speak of. Constantine's laconic answer – "Magic" – does not really help us readers understand how he managed to scare away dozens of beings more powerful than himself. A similar moment takes place in the movie *Constantine*, as Constantine is fighting the demon Balthazar and threatening to subdue the evil entity in the most ironic and, as such, frightening way – absolving Balthazar's sins and sending him to heaven. Here, as well, Constantine gets what he wants by defeating the demon without fulfilling his threats and without employing any special power.

At least in the movie, we see that indeed, Constantine does not possess any meaningful direct power against demons, even if he does have some abilities that will be discussed later. However, he is indeed privileged with an important advantage that helps him conclude his ordeals with the upper hand. This ability is his knowledge of the strict metaphysical rules of existence, as well as the occult gnosis of setting his sails to their winds in the right way, overcoming obstacles and enemies by doing so. This is hardly a unique case for either a hero or an anti-hero in a movie. However, the cinematic character of John Constantine, to be examined here, is but one manifestation of the same archetypal idea taking place in three different cinematic worlds. These worlds are connected to each other not only through this form of reading, along with the symbolism that will be further unfolded here, but also through the main fictional characters, portrayed by the same actor, Keanu Reeves. Indeed, if we are living in an era in which mythology is constantly nurtured though the screen — in addition to numerous other mythologies, if not altogether through the digital media — then the actors, whose prerogative is to alter the viewers' perception according to the twists and turns of the cinematic mythology, cannot be completely detached from the characters they portray. In this form of dream interpretation, and through the trinity of Reeves' manifestations, we can examine the triple, parallel worlds of the magician as he appears in the movies *Constantine* (Lawrence, 2005), *The Matrix* trilogy (Wachowski & Wachowski, 1999, 2003, 2003) and *John Wick* (Stahelski, 2014, 2017, 2019, 2023).

Each of the three movies deals with a similar story about a world that is locked within a firm set of rules at its very core, and the magician who manages to manipulate and break these rules. However, these worlds vary in their metaphysics, cosmogony and the temporal direction that paves the way for the magician. The world of *Constantine* is a world in which God and the devil are battling for dominance over an otherwise material, albeit Catholic world of man. In this world, John Constantine's battle is against his future fate. Constantine is a heavy smoker who suffers from terminal lung cancer. As a teenager he tried to commit suicide and effectively died for two minutes before being resuscitated. Thus, Constantine is facing the judgement of two different sets of rules: biological rules, according to which he will soon die from cancer, and metaphysical rules, according to which he is destined to suffer in hell for all eternity, for the spiritual crime of committing suicide. When he meets the Angel Gabriel for the first time in the movie, Gabriel explains his situation to him by saying: "You are going to die young because you smoked 30 cigarettes a day since you were 15 ... and you're going to go to hell because of the life you took. You're fucked."

The world of *Constantine* is vivid with Catholic symbolism and mythology. It's main object of interest is the artefact known as the spear of destiny, with which Christ was killed while being hanged on the cross. The rules of the earthly world are, as already mentioned, Catholic. Angels, as well as demons, have a central, albeit indirect role in the lives of humans. In the world of *John Wick*, however, we see a world in which God is long dead, while the symbolism that has defined his worship for so many centuries remains even in his absence. This is a world in which society is being heavily infiltrated not by celestial or demonic entities, but by social entities — meaning numerous underworld criminal organizations — all locked with and against each other in a balance of power and ruled by a bureaucratic body titled "The High Table." In this world, rules are everything. In a godless world, these rules — as mentioned on numerous occasions throughout the four *John Wick* movies — are what separates the world of mankind from the rest of the animal kingdom. The movie begins with the introduction of Wick as a retired hitman who lives peacefully outside the criminal system. He is then violently pulled back into the underworld by an act of brutal violence, as Iosef Tarasov, whose father Viggo Tarasov is the head of the Russian mafia in New York, kills his dog and steals his car. What begins as Wicks' unconditional revenge against the people who attacked him and killed his dog, ends up with him becoming an extreme challenge for the entire underworld. In the past, when Wick was employed as a hitman by Viggo and asked to retire, he was given an impossible mission by Viggo in order to be permitted to retire — a mission Wick, an initiate to the afterworldly freedom from the grip of the underworld, managed to complete successfully. Now, as a menace to the entire underworld system, which is united and set against him, Wick himself becomes a danger to the world more than the world is a danger for Wick. One can watch the four *John Wick* movies and recall the moment in Alan Moore's graphic novel *Watchmen*,[2] in which Walter Joseph Kovacs, known as the anti-hero Rorschach, is locked in jail together with the dozens of criminals he himself caught and handed over to the police. While the inmates believe that this is a golden opportunity for their long-awaited revenge on Kovacs, they quickly discover that it is not him who is in danger, but them. As he is being dragged away by the prison guards after pouring burning oil on the face of another inmate who tried to attack him, Kovacs yells: "None of you seem to understand. I'm not locked in here with you... you're locked in here with me!"[3]

Wick left the underworld in order to live peacefully with his wife Helen, who then died tragically, leaving him his dog as a final memory from her. After Iosef Tarasov kills the dog, Wick does not only avenge the dog's death, but more importantly for him, the now-lost memory of his dead wife. Otherwise, he has very little to live for. When asked, Wick replies that he only lives in order to maintain the memory of Helen, and so if Constantine waged war against hell in order to change the future, Wick wages war against the underworld in order to avenge the past and to remember it. On a broader scope, this seems like the kind of a mission that this entire godless world has taken upon itself. Not only are the various hitmen, including Wick, adorned with religious tattoos and artefacts (more than others, perhaps, is Wick's home clan in Berlin — The Ruska Roma — whose symbolism is of orthodox Christianity), but also their entire lexicon is as religious as much as it is bureaucratic. At one time, for instance, Wick is being excommunicated. On another occasion, The Continental Hotel — a neutral establishment to be discussed later on — is destroyed in a procedure that is titled Deconsecration.

Finally, in the world of Neo in *The Matrix*, God returns, or perhaps he re-emerges, as a Gnostic demiurge that has created a false, virtual prison world for mankind. Neo begins as Thomas A. Anderson, the son of Michelle McGahey and — if to complete the trinity of holy names as well, joining John Constantine and John Wick — John Anderson. Anderson works as a programmer, as well as being a hacker involved in illegal activities. He then learns, with the help of several mysterious figures, that he, like the rest of humanity, actually lives in a shattered world controlled by machines who breed and grow humans in individual incubator cells; the humans live their lives within a virtual simulation that they believe to be the real world. Having this knowledge and having escaped this virtual world, Anderson returns to the matrix as Neo, the one, in order to save humanity and shatter the walls of this virtual Plato's cave.

Unlike the virtual world, which only seems to be real and present-day, the real world in *The Matrix* is not only a dark, shattered world, but it is also displaced temporally. Since the matrix is programmed to simulate late twentieth-century Earth, in the perspective of Neo the real world is in the future, decades after the simulated time inside the matrix. Once he is aware that the world that he knew is nothing but a virtual simulation, the point of the present moment shifts in his understanding of the historical timeline through which he lives. When Morpheus, who ritualistically baptizes Neo into the real reality, reveals the truth about the world to Neo for the first time, he does it through a virtual simulation of the real world, while saying "Welcome to the desert of the real," echoing the philosopher Jean Baudrillard, whose seminal book *Simulacra and Simulation* serves Neo as a mock imitation of a book in which he hides illegal computer parts in the beginning of the movie. While the various references to Baudrillard in *The Matrix* should indeed be discussed, Morpheus' declaration may be read more in the spirit of the words "Abandon all hope, ye who enter here," inscribed above the gates of hell in Dante's *Inferno*. The real world is a desert, not only because it has become alien to any possible human meaning, once conquered by the machines, but it has also become an underworld – an infrastructure for the seeding, growing, and harvesting of humanity in its virtual prison. This real world is dark and mechanical, with no remains for a transcendent godly symbolism besides the last hidden city of Zion, buried close to the core of the Earth. This is the satanic inversion of the celestial hierarchy, as imagined by the demon Mammon, the son of Lucifer in *Constantine*. The inhuman underworld (or infrastructure) has taken over the Earth, the celestial world is no more, remaining only as a virtual mockery of itself, and the living, free humanity driven down under to the bowels of the Earth. As if to ensure that no real celestial interference will ever interrupt the reign of the machine demons, the sky was scorched, and the Earth is now eternally covered by an impenetrable layer of dark clouds of unknowing the heavens. This desperate action was made by the humans in their war against the machine, as if to signify the ultimate sin of abandoning the sky, the rest of the universe and God. In the new war against the machines, a war that is now led by Neo, he and his companion, whose name is Trinity, fly and penetrate for a brief moment through the thick layer of the dark clouds. In this moment, they see a different world. They see the sun shining brightly in the calm sky, majestic and oblivious to the horrific reality on the face of the Earth. At this moment, the true Gnostic reality of the universe is revealed. The ancient Gnostic beliefs, whether Judeo-Christian or Pagan, implies a conspiracy to imprison humanity within a false, material world. This scheme is performed by the Demiurge, which is believed to be the one true god, although he is an evil entity. The true god, the true Sophia, is distant and almost oblivious to mankind, as it is the mission of the Gnostic to reunite with this true deity,[4] — a mission briefly understood by Neo and Trinity.

Neo, then, is christened in order to fight for the true present and to distinguish it from the false, virtual and simulated present. His newfound knowledge of the world and of himself allows him to move between the worlds. He enters the false world in which mankind is imprisoned, achieving superhuman powers through the occult knowledge of how to alter the very metaphysics of the simulated reality by hacking its algorithms. He can now understand the metaphysics of the real, mechanical world, and so come in touch with its demiurge in order to liberate mankind. Like Constantine and Wick, Neo is also able to free mankind from its shackles because he knows and understands the rules — both of the physical and the virtual realities — and so he can transcend the laws of the virtual and maneuver successfully through the laws of the physical.

In the worlds of Constantine and Wick, worlds that are either fought over by God, or still have traces of his worship, the protagonists are both heroes and antiheroes at the same time. As their will, and should we allow ourselves to use a more Newtonian metaphor — their force of will — remains constant at all times, they shift between being a hero and being an antihero through their odysseys. For Neo the hero, it takes a longer time to learn and to come to terms with his abilities and purpose in life, and so we witness his complete transformation from the bored, cynical programmer to the very savior of the world. Be that as it may, all three characters are transitioning, either constantly or just once, throughout the three movies, between two different phases. In relation to the world, we can see different metaphysical formulations of the protagonists, formulations that may be compared to those offered by the nineteenth-century magician, Éliphas Lévi.

In his *Transcendental Magic,* Lévi discusses the magical interpretation of the movement from unity to the duad, from the duad to the trinity and then to the tetragram – the equilibrium of the trinity with its new-founded unification. The tetragrammaton – God, for instance, as Lévi describes him – is not merely a unity, but a unity that emerges from the three persons in God, meaning the father, the son and the holy spirit.[5] In this way we can distinguish between Constantine, Wick and Neo. Constantine is one and alone, never growing or diffusing beyond his own singularity and loneliness. In his godless world, Wick is the new, carnal trinity. He is the holy spirit, being called *The Baba Yaga,* who comes back to punish the criminal world, as the father, Viggo Tarasov, sends his son to him in order to awaken him and make his loss vivid again. Thus, becoming a trinity, Wick is still missing a part of himself, or else he would not enter the world and change it. Finally, Neo, while declared as the one, is awakened and christened by Morpheus, and joined by the trinity he becomes a complete, seemingly omnipotent being in the virtual world, thus saving mankind from the manipulative system that has set borders to it.

Unlike many of their allies, enemies and acquaintances, Constantine, Wick and Neo are indeed men who can act in their world, thus manipulating and changing it for their own ends, for the benefit of their friends or for the sake of all mankind. In understanding these three holy quests, we can now delve into a more detailed examination not only of the magician himself, but of the ceremonial items that he employs. Then, we can finally stand against the demons that are in the magician's way.

Notes

1. Bruno, Giordano, *Cause, Principle and Unity: And Essays on Magic,* Richard J. Blackwell and Robert de Luca (trans.). Cambridge: Cambridge University Press, 2004.
2. Moore, Alan and Gibbons, Dave, *Watchmen*. New York: DC Comics, 1987.
3. Ibid., p. 186.

4. Jonas, Hans, *The Gnostic Religion: The Message of the Alien God and the Beginning of Christianity*. Boston: Beacon Press, 1991.
5. Lévi, Éliphas, *Transcendental Magic: Its Doctrine and Ritual*, Arthur Edward Waite (trans.). Mansfield Centre: Martino Publishing, 2011, pp. 53-62.

2.

Totems and Familiars

> "There's nothing in here really worth stealing, but if anything were taken it would cost me a tremendous amount of trouble to replace it, no matter how worthless it would prove to the thief. Also, there's the problem of contamination — just one ignorant touch could destroy the work of months. It's rather like a bacteriology laboratory in that respect. Hence the Guardian."
>
> "Obviously there can't be a standard supply house for your tools," Hess agreed, recovering his composure.
>
> "No, that's not even theoretically possible. The operator must make everything himself — not as easy now as it was in the Middle Ages, when most educated men had the requisite skills as a matter of course. Here we go."
>
> James Blish, *Black Easter.*[1]

Sulphur, Quicksilver and Salt

In 1999, the year in which *The Matrix* was released, a short story called *1408* was published by Stephen King, later to become a movie bearing the same name, released in 2007. In this movie we follow Mike Enslin, a cynical and skeptical author of books, in which he describes his visits to numerous sites, provocatively dubbed as "haunted." Enslin does not believe in ghosts, nor does he think that the places he visits might be haunted. However, he does carry whatever devices he thinks are necessary for him in order to be able to recognize an unnatural event, should he ever find himself in one. Most advanced in his inventory are EMF readers and infrared vision equipment, but Enslin's two most personal items are his mini-cassette recorder, which allows him to constantly record his thoughts and findings, and a cigarette. As Enslin explains to the owner of the one truly haunted place that he discovers in his life, the Dolphin Hotel, Enslin does not usually smoke. Yet wherever he goes, he brings a cigarette as a ritualistic talisman to every potentially haunted site he visits, without actually lighting it. *1408* is a story about Enslin's encounter with a supernatural room, room number 1408 in the Dolphin Hotel. At the climax of the movie, when he is almost defeated by the room — not a haunted room, but rather an evil room — Enslin finally lights his cigarette.

Enslin's character brings to mind that of Constantine, with his cynicism and venomous sense of irony. Unlike Enslin, however, Constantine is not skeptical of the supernatural. As the Angel Gabriel points out, Constantine does not merely believe in the world of demons and angels, he *knows* about it, and he is familiar with it. Constantine, then, does not have to wait for the lowest point in his encounters with the supernatural, in order to smoke. Constantine smokes constantly. The ongoing smoking ritual works not only as Constantine's incidental habit that both relieves the stress accumulated through the constant dealing with the underworld and hastens Constantine's demise and afterlife in that very same place, it also, perhaps in a more symbolic sense, mirrors the microcosm and the macrocosm through the flesh and blood conduit that is Constantine. Several times in the movie, he connects the smell of burning sulfur with the presence of demons or with a similar ecology of hell. It is not known whether the smell of burning sulpher is a byproduct of the presence of demons, a part of the hellish atmosphere or perhaps even a sign of the demons' ability to poison their surroundings. The presence of burning sulphur, however, is the medium through which demons erupt — both on Earth and in hell. In a similar way to Constantine's battle against the exterior, meaning the hellish demons that endanger mankind, the burning smoke of the cigarettes, this ceremonial incense taken inwards, is the medium through which Constantine's cancerous demons emerge within his own body. Both demons – those beyond nature and those a grim consequence of it – threaten with the same purpose for Constantine's after life.

In one scene, seconds before Constantine's surprise attack on Balthazar, we see the human-like demon examining a mirror in front of him, as it seems to melt and boil. Prior to any sense of heat or to any physical damage that might have been inflicted through the blast of the glass, there is the moment in which the image of Balthazar is distorted and no longer represents himself in the same accuracy we usually demand from mirrors (hence the traditional fear from the vampire's lack of a mirror image). Such accuracy is both a blessing and a curse, as John Wick discovers during one of his numerous epic battles throughout the *John Wick* saga, now taking place in a maze of mirrors, through which he needs to discern real enemies from their mere mirror images.

Much more to the spirit of the mirror scene in *Constantine,* however, is the scene in *The Matrix,* in which Neo touches a mirror that not only reveals itself to be liquid, but it also penetrates Neo's body and then completely merges with him, thus allowing a virtual transformation through which Neo is now able to see through the many worlds – one physical and the rest virtual. This kind of mirror, then, is a liquid metaphysical gate that is frozen in a solid, fragile state, and is not limited to *The Matrix,* of course. Similar mirrors served as gateways to other worlds for Alice, as she discovered and explored Wonderland, for instance. These other worlds can also serve as spaces of imprisonment, such as the one used by Constantine in the beginning of the movie, as he performs an act of exorcism and forces a demon out of the body of a young girl and into a mirror, shattering it afterwards and thus sending the demon back to hell.

By looking at such mirrors shown in the three movies, we learn that the image shown through the reflecting surface may not be a mere reflection, but some-*one*, some-*thing* or some-*place* else. These mirrors, however, need a host, meaning someone to look at them, in order for the mirror to function as a form of an Other. Gaze is an invitation to action. Thus, we hear Constantine's warning, twice throughout the movie, not to look. The first warning takes place in the act of exorcism, when Constantine warns the people who help him not to open their eyes, no matter what happens. One of them cannot overcome the temptation, so we see, and is rapidly aged before dying seconds later. The second time takes place when Constantine and Detective Angela Dodson encounter a horde of demons (preceded by the inevitable stench of sulphur) in the street. Angela opens her eyes as well and is stricken with horror at the sight of the countless demonic beings above her head. In a similar way, in *John Wick*, tremendous shooting scenes take place in public spaces and among the crowd who do not look and appear not to notice them at all. In *The Matrix*, the people who can see through the artificial and virtual reality wear sunglasses, blocking the sight of their gaze from the rest of the population.

Given their alchemical values, both sulphur and quicksilver (here represented by the mirror) are signifiers for the other realm, another side, be it the supernatural or the virtual, in *Constantine* and *The Matrix*. Not to delve into the long history of alchemical significance of these two materials, we can think of the importance of the unfathomable other, be it theological or technological, through the description of the fifteenth-century alchemist Basilius Valentinus, who considered sulphur and quicksilver to be the components of every metal — sulphur being spirit and quicksilver being soul.[2] This is a comparison we can agree with, considering the journey of the spirit in

Constantine and the detachment of the soul from the physical world in *The Matrix*. There is, however, a third component to metals, according to Valentinus, which is salt, meaning the body.[3] The body is all that remains in *John Wick*. Whatever burns exists in this world — be it buildings or people; whatever seen through the mirror exists here and now — be it Wick's enemies or even his own body, as he sews stitches in himself through the use of such a mirror after being shot.

In this scene, after being excommunicated from the rest of the underworld with a prize on his head, Wick needs to sew a bullet wound after a doctor is not able to help him any longer without consequences, as the excommunication is activated in the middle of Wick's surgery. In a world in which God is dead, and a humanist regime of an underworld is all there is; in a world in which all that matters for Wick is the memory of his dead wife Helen, as more and more antagonists attempt to rob him of his life and of his memories, the extraction of bullets is an act of a material exorcism. In other words, the bullet that is buried in Wick's body is a growing threat that endangers not only Wick himself, but also the last remains of any form of transcendence — the memory of the dead — and so needs to be removed.

We see similar incidents both in *Constantine* and *The Matrix*. The movie *Constantine* begins with John Constantine exorcising a demon out of the body of a young girl, in attempts to rob her of her soul. In *The Matrix*, Neo himself goes through a technological exorcism, as a parasite, squid-like robot is taken out of his body. This exorcism is, we then discover, a part of the process in which Neo's soul, meaning his *self*, is finally reunited with his material body outside the matrix.

Grimoires and Non-Human Companions

In the beginning of *The Divine Comedy*, Dante's epic and complex elaboration of the nine circles of hell, his journey begins not with the explicit will to venture into the underworld, together with his guide, Virgil, but in an attempt to escape the ordeal altogether. In his attempt to walk in a different direction, Dante encounters a wild beast that stands in his way, and so is forced to turn back, as we read the words:

> Behold the beast, for which I have turned back;
> Do thou protect me from her, famous Sage,
> For she doth make my veins and pulses tremble.[4]

In fact, we can say it is the beast that sends Dante on his quest, or rather forces him onwards. In a similar way, we can see the appearances of various animals that share a similar purpose in the three stories — one transcendental, one immanent and one virtual. As Constantine helps Angela and ventures into hell in order to try and locate her sister, he does so with the help of her black cat, explaining that "They're half in and half out anyway." In *John Wick,* it is the merciless murder of his dog that sends Wick to an all-out war against the entire underworld, as the dog is Wick's last vivid memory of his wife. At the end of the first *John Wick* movie, Wick finds himself in an animal shelter. He then takes one of the dogs that are being kept there, adopting him as a new animal companion. In *The Matrix*, it is a black cat that signifies a glitch in the matrix and the updating of a change throughout the virtual world, both in *The Matrix 1* and at the end of *The Matrix 3*. Another notable distinction is that of these animals' names. The cats in *The Matrix* are not related to any human, but rather they are totem representations of the living, virtual world changing itself. Being symbolic avatars of this world, these cats are distant, uncaring and do not really interact with humans. Wick's dog, as shown from the end of the first movie onwards, is a friendly dog that Wick refuses to name, and so the dog remains nameless, referred to only as "dog" — a man-made signifier for this animal, but a general one, lacking any man-made individuality. In *Constantine,* Angela's cat is called "Duck," thus breaking, albeit comically, whatever mythological metaphors that might accompany a black cat that is halfway through to hell.

In the three movies, the animal behaves as a conduit to a different world, without which it would be either difficult or impossible for the protagonist to witness the infrastructure that connects between the worlds, or better yet travel through them. Another such instrument is either one of the three books appearing in the three stories, each carrying with it a different occult truth. It would be almost pointless to discuss the history of grimoires and other forms of written metaphysical secrets, as such a detour from our subject of inquiry would prove to be immense.[5] However, a cinematic reference that should be mentioned is Roman Polanski's *The Ninth Gate,* in which Dean Corso (Johnny Depp) is a book dealer who specializes in rare books and is looking for clues regarding a seventeenth-century book titled "The Nine Gates of the Kingdom of Shadows," which is said to be a great magical work by which the devil himself can be summoned. In this movie, the book appears not merely as a singular source of occult information, but rather as an unholy trinity of books, each containing only a part of the information needed to prepare the correct ceremony by which the devil can be summoned. Although looking quite identical, Corso finds out that they differ slightly in the images shown in them. In this movie, Corso can remind us, in some of his characteristics, of Constantine, Wick and in a darker sense, Neo. Like Constantine, Corso is a very cynical person and as a book dealer, cares only about material profit and has very little interest in anything else. Unlike Constantine, though, Corso believes neither in magic nor in the devil, and blatantly mocks those around him who do. For the most part of the movie, Corso lives in a world without God, without the devil and without magic, although his world, much like Wick's godless world, is vivid with such symbolism — magical and satanic. Perhaps, by reading the aforementioned symbolism in *Constantine,* as well as in *1408,* we can tell that Corso, even as a firm nonbeliever, really deals with the supernatural and the demonic as he is constantly shown smoking a cigarette in many, if not most, of the scenes in the movie. Ultimately, much like Neo but in a darker, more sinister way, Corso discovers another world, that of demons and the devil, and gains unearthly power over it. He has sex with a peculiar woman he met in the beginning of the movie — a woman who is then revealed to be a demonic succubus — and he acquires the last part of the dark book, by which he himself could summon the devil, or so we understand.

Through the occult book, Corso gains a better understanding of a more complex reality by the end of the movie. That is not the case in the three movies that we examine, however. In *Constantine, John Wick* and *The Matrix,* the books shown in each of the movies merely offer the viewers clues about the world in which the protagonists live. In this sense, the books — even when not dealing strictly with the occult world — are books of the occult. If in *The Ninth Gate* we saw a book that exists as a trinity rather than a singular source of knowledge, then in *Constantine* we discover that the New Testament's *Corinthians* indeed has a secret, mirrored image of it in hell — a copy in which there is a seventeenth chapter that does not exist in the earthly version of the book. When Constantine discovers a reference to this chapter, he then understands the plot of the demon Mammon, the son of the devil, to take control over the world of humans. In other words, the book does not offer Constantine power, but rather a piece of information about the demonic plot to take over the world.

The other two books, seen in *The Matrix* and in *John Wick,* are not actual books that are intended for reading, but rather hollowed out books, in which Neo and Wick hide certain objects that are valuable for them. In the beginning of the first movie of *The Matrix,* we see that Neo hides some suspicious software inside the book *Simulacra and Simulation* by Jean Baudrillard,[6] while Wick hides money and his clan's religious symbol of membership in the book *Russian Folk Tale* by Alexander Afanasyev.[7] Since both these books serve as covers for hidden objects and not as books, their textual content seems not to be referred to directly in the movies. However, and as one can expect, each of these books adds a distinct meaning to the movie it appears in. The most important references in Afanasyev's *Russian Folk Tale,* in the context of the movie *John Wick,* are the three stories "Baba Yaga," "Prince Danila-Govorila" and "The Little White Duck," three stories that tell tales of the witch Baba Yaga — a title that is given to John Wick as well, for his seemingly inhuman resourcefulness, endurance and invulnerability. However, there are more folk stories in this compendium that can help uncover the metaphysics of Wick's world and storyline. The story of "The Little Hen," for instance, begins with an incident that ends up as a cataclysmic disaster that engulfs the entire clerical hierarchy, as this story is described by the translator, Sergey Levchin.[8] Taken to the context of the rigid hierarchy portrayed in the four *John Wick* movies, we can see how a symbolic, even if violent, incident in the beginning of the first movie, sets in motion nothing short of a global political cataclysm.

The Matrix references to Baudrillard's philosophy do not end with *Simulacra and Simulation* shown at the beginning of the movie. We, like Neo, are introduced to "The desert of the real," which is also a Baudrillardian idea, as we learn about the matrix, a virtual representation of the world. *Simulacra and Simulation* opens with Baudrillard referring to Jorges Louis Borges' story of the cartographers designing a map so precise in its description of the territory, that the people begin to live on it, rather than on their land.[9] We can see, then, the similarities between the ideas expressed by Baudrillard to those shown in

The Matrix. However, when asked about the movie, Baudrillard saw numerous flaws in the cinematic attempt to refer to his philosophy. In an interview with *Le Nouvel Observateur*, Baudrillard said that:

> already there have been other films that treat the growing indistinction between the real and the virtual: *The Truman Show, Minority Report,* or even *Mulholland Drive,* the masterpiece of David Lynch. *The Matrix*'s value is chiefly as a synthesis of all that. But there the set-up is cruder and does not truly evoke the problem. The actors are in the matrix, that is, in the digitized system of things; or, they are radically outside it, such as in Zion, the city of resistors. But what would be interesting is to show what happens when these two worlds collide. The most embarrassing part of the film is that the new problem posed by simulation is confused with its classical, Platonic treatment. This is a serious flaw. The radical illusion of the world is a problem faced by all great cultures, which they have solved through art and symbolization. What we have invented, in order to support this suffering, is a simulated real, which henceforth supplants the real and is its final solution, a virtual universe from which everything dangerous and negative has been expelled. And *The Matrix* is undeniably part of that. Everything belonging to the order of dream, utopia and phantasm is given expression, "realized." We are in the uncut transparency. *The Matrix* is surely the kind of film about the matrix that the matrix would have been able to produce.[10]

Simulacra and Simulation deals with the loss of the real in favor of a simulacra that either replaces it or stands for something that never was real in the first place. In this sense, something interesting happens in the interaction between the viewer and the movie, rather than as a part of the movie storyline. It is the movie, an obvious product of the entertainment industry, which not only makes people around the world think that they are actually living in a digital simulation, but it also sets a fictious movie as an example for people opening their eyes to reality.

In other words, among the numerous cultural effects that *The Matrix* has, two effects change the way in which some of us see the world. The first one is the diffusion of the belief that, well, we in fact live inside a virtual simulation, rather than in the "real" world. In its essence, this belief is not necessarily new. The idea that a transcendental God created a world, that he as a god exists outside of, is very similar to the idea that our own world was artificially created by beings — either humans, machines or aliens, that exist outside its borders. The belief in a simulated world, thus, brings back the creationist view on the emergence of the world, with one crucial difference. The creators of the world in *The Matrix,* as well as in the theory of the simulated world, are immanent to the material world, even if it lies beyond the borders of our smaller, virtual world. In this case, not only are we subjects to the whims of an entity that has complete power over our existence, but also this entity is material in the sense that we are material and therefore it does not have any transcendent aspiration for our existence. In essence, the possibility that our world is a simulation means that it is being controlled by *Someone,* like us in a way, who has complete power over our existence, knowledge, beliefs, will, etc. In this world, what we then have to do is to learn how to see the world for what it truly is, rather than as the way it is artificially presented to us. This simulated world, then, is the revival or continuation of the Gnostic belief in a false world, created by an evil demiurge far from the reach of the ever-transcendent reach of true godliness.

The other effect this movie has, which echoes not only Baudrillard's philosophy, but also his statement that "*The Matrix* is surely the kind of film about the matrix that the matrix would have been able to produce," is how quickly we began using the phrase "To get out of the matrix" in order to express the idea of "waking up"; of breaking the Platonic shackles of the artificial, orchestrated and malicious representation of what we thought was reality, and finally seeing the world for what it really is. The irony should be evident — not only that Neo has no way to find out if what he now thinks is the real world, the shattered world that is controlled by the machines, is indeed the real world, but also in order to express our reconnection with naked reality, we use a phrase that comes from the cinematic industry, which in its essence (and also according to the Platonic thought!) takes us farther away from truth and from reality. An ouroboros.

Holy Weapons and Magic Shields

The three aforementioned acts of exorcism (of demons in *Constantine*, of robots in *The Matrix* and of bullets in *John Wick*) cannot but remind us of another such exorcism cinematic saga, that of *Alien*. In this series of movies, the horrific alien species of Xenomorphs lay eggs inside other living beings, only for them to hatch from within the living, suffering beings, killing them in the process. In the movie *ALIEN 3* (Fincher, 1992), we see a scene in which the Xenomorph mother's monstrous face almost touches that of the helpless protagonist, Ellen Ripley, only to then spare her life and leave. This scene, reminiscent of the numerous paintings of Judas' kiss to Jesus, informing the Roman soldiers of his identity and portraying the ultimate act of betrayal, can also be seen in our topics of discussion. In the climax of *Constantine*, the devil approaches the dying detective in such manner, in a similar way in which Agent Smith approaches the suffering Morpheus in *The Matrix*. In these scenes, perhaps implying that an ultimate act of betrayal is possible only within the boundaries of the ultimate battle between good and evil, we are witnessing the war of wars, the unholy and ultimate threat to mankind.

Such unholy wars demand the use of the right holy weaponry, as seen in each of the three movies, in each of which the protagonist is supplied with the right armament in a middle ground that seems detached from the rest of the world, before embarking on his quest. In *Constantine,* John Constantine visits both Beeman in a separate room inside the bowling alley, and Papa Midnite's bar, which will be discussed later, in order to obtain weaponry and protection. John Wick visits numerous secret stores, in which weapons and special protection suits are made for his needs, and if the devices in *Constantine* have their religious or mythical connotations to their names, in *John Wick* the equipment is sold through a strictly symbolic language code that gives hints for their tactical usage, such as "formal event suits" or "social affair suits," both terms referring to different forms of armed combat. In *The Matrix,* Neo receives his weapons from a virtual middle ground that is both a part of the matrix and exterior to the simulation of the earthly world. In essence, his equipment emerges from the very fabric of the reality he is fighting against, much like the weaponry used by Constantine, having a portion of holiness in them, as required in the battle between the holy and the unholy. In both worlds, that of *The Matrix* and that of *John Wick* (in the third *John Wick* movie), a similar scene takes place. Neo enters the white middle ground, while Wick enters Winston's secret room, both having a similar request before going on their important mission — "Guns."

Each story has its own form of a talisman of protection against the specific forces of evil who threaten the world. While in *Constantine,* this talisman is indeed a magical talisman that Constantine gives Angela in order to protect her from the malicious forces of darkness, *The Matrix* and *John Wick* both offer less literal magical talismans. Like every other being, human or virtual, who knows that the world of the matrix is a mere virtual fabrication of reality, Neo wears black sunglasses whenever he visits the matrix. This simple apparatus, while not explicitly discussed in the movie, is an inevitable reference to an earlier cinematic appearance of a matrix. That matrix is of a simulated world that hides a terrible, dark truth beneath it, and can be found in the movie *They Live* (Carpenter, 1988), in which the protagonist finds special sunglasses through which he is able to see the world for what it truly is, rather than the way it appears to be. If in *The Matrix*, the virtual world has a strong greenish digital hue to it, the real world in the movie *They Live* is seen through a black and white filter, rather than in color. In other words, there is a clear distinction between the false world and the real world — a difference that is shown through the visual spectrum, even though the meaning of this difference is reversed in the two movies. In the movie *They Live*, the protagonist cannot see the real world fully for what it truly is, but only through a sight-limiting black and white filter, while in *The Matrix*, it is the false world that is essentially limited in its visual representation, pushed towards a greenish hue rather than a richer spectrum of colors.

The magical talismans in *John Wick*, meaning the numerous religious icons that Wick uses throughout the *John Wick* saga, together with medallions of debt between him and other mercenaries, are used in order to postpone the procedural reality that is quickly closing in on Wick through strict rules, regulations and orders. In Wick's world, devoid of any god whatsoever, theological or virtual, in a world in which man-made rules are all there is, Wick's inventory of protection equipment is indeed similar only to a magician's ability to deny reality even if for a short period of time.

Notes

1. Blish, James, *The Devil's Day*. New York: Baen Publishing Enterprises, 1971, p. 37.
2. Burckhardt, Titus, *Alchemy: Science of the Cosmos, Science of the Soul*, William Stoddart (trans.). Baltimore: Penguin Books, 1972, p. 139.
3. Ibid.
4. Dante, Alighieri, Amari-Parker, Anna (ed.), *Dante's Divine Comedy: Hell, Purgatory, Paradise*, Henry W. Longfellow (trans.). London: Arcturus Publishing Limited, 2006, Canto I, p. 16.
5. Two examples for books that deal with the history and writing of grimoires are: Davis, Owen, *Grimoires: A History of Magic Books* (Oxford: Oxford University Press, 2009) and Lecouteux, Claude, *The Book of Grimoires: The Secret Grammar of Magic*, Jon E. Graham (trans.) (Rochester: Inner Traditions, 2013).
6. For a contemporary version of this book, see Baudrillard, Jean, *Simulacra and Simulation*, Sheila Faria Glaser, Ann Arbor (trans.). The University of Michigan Press, 2017.
7. For reference, I used this book: Afanasyv, Alexander, *Russian Folk Tale: A Dual Language Book*, Sergey Levchin (trans.). Mineola: Dover Publishing, 2014.
8. Ibid., p. 11.
9. Baudrillard, Jean, *Simulacra and Simulation*, Sheila Faria Glaser, Ann Arbor (trans.) The University of Michigan Press, 2017, p. 1.
10. https://baudrillardstudies.ubishops.ca/the-matrix-decoded-le-nouvel-observateur-interview-with-jean-baudrillard/.

3.

Exile, Sacrifice and Resistance

Baroness Kessler: "I saw him one day. I was fifteen years old, and I saw him as plain as I see you now. It was love at first sight."
Dean Corso: "You know, 300 years ago, you'd have been burned at the stake for saying something like that."
Baroness Kessler: "300 years ago I wouldn't have said it!"

The Ninth Gate (Polanski, 1999).

Ever since the Platonic emergence from the cave, the blindness — in his case, by the shear brightness of the illuminating sun — could be thought of not as a curse, but as a blessing. In Plato's allegory of the cave, if to tell it in brief outlines, a man who lived his entire life in a cave, seeing only shadows moving across the wall, thinks that these shadows are real objects. He then escapes his shackles, leaves his fellows and wanders around the cave. Looking around the cave, he sees other people who move statues around a great fire. Realizing the nature of the shadows he saw, he then concludes that these statues are the real objects, while the shadows were just that — their shadows. But then he discovers the opening of the cave and goes outside. Leaving the cave behind, he sees the material world and acknowledges that indeed this is the real world and everything else he saw before was mere reductions of it — reductions into a spiral of various atrophied representations. Before finally seeing the world outside, though, this man is blinded by the sun's light. Having lived inside the cave for his entire life, this blindness resets his understanding of reality, to the point that without this purification process, he could not have achieved the knowledge of what is real. Blindness clears our false conceptions of the world.

We see this in the graphic novel *The Books of Magic*, taking place in the world of John Constantine. The protagonist of this story, the child Timothy, is taken to the very distant future by one of Constantine's acquaintances. The enigmatic Mister E. E. is blind and, as he describes it, he can see good and evil, and nothing else. In other words, Mr. E. would say that he does not see the falsities of the world anymore, but only its absolutes. He then tells the story of how he was blinded by his father, who caught him looking at erotic pictures of women as a child. His answer to Timothy's disgust from the story is a quote from Matthew, chapter 18, verse 9: "If thine eye offend thee, pluck it out, and cast it from thee: It is better for thee to enter into life with one eye, rather than having two eyes and be cast into hell fire."[1]

In *John Wick 4*, Wick's nemesis and friend, Caine, is a formidable, albeit blind assassin. Rather than letting the high table take his sight by force, he blinds himself in order to protect his daughter, and more importantly — as we witness in the movie — his blindness does not make him less capable as an assassin, but rather a better one. Shutting down his sense of sight sharpens his other senses, especially his hearing. Closing in to the final climax of *The Matrix*, Neo is also hit in his eyes by a physical attack from the virtual agent, Smith, who takes over, possesses his friend in the real world, rendering Neo blind. Neo is far from remaining incapable, however. Blinded in the normal sense, he can now sense both the matrix and the real world much clearer, thus suggesting, in a way, that there might be an even wider matrix that is locking everything — human and machine — in.

Alongside these avatars of changes in the perceptions of reality, there is also a symbolic, demonological triangle, spectrally haunting the story line in each of the three movies. The three points of this triangle are the existence of a neutral zone, the ever-diminishing presence of humans in the world, and the emergence of alien cities. In *Constantine,* John Constantine visits Papa Midnite's bar twice. Within the ongoing, hidden proxy war between angels and demons in the world of humans, Papa Midnite holds a powerful position of owning a neutral bar, a stable stronghold in which both beings of light and of darkness are welcome, and in which no hostility between the two sides is allowed. Indeed, the sovereignty of the establishment, based on Midnite's presence and power, manifests itself through the complete prohibition of violence or any other use of force. When Constantine breaks this first law of Midnite's bar, he is severely punished. Constantine, however, breaks the rule for a justified reason. While Midnite's ideology is of complete neutrality, Constantine shows him how the balance was actually broken without Midnite's awareness.

A similar incident takes place in the movie *John Wick,* within the premises of the ever-neutral Continental Hotel, to which all assassins and members of the man-made, social underworld are welcome, and in which no act of violence is ever allowed. In the first movie, an attempt on Wick's life within the premises of the hotel is followed by the swift execution of the woman who tried to kill him, as soon as she walks outside the establishment. The power and sovereignty of the Continental Hotel is ever present, willing and quick to respond to any attempt to break its rule. Later on in the saga, John Wick himself shoots Santino D'Antonio, despite the clear warnings of Winston Scott, the manager of the hotel who is present in the room with Wick and D'Antonio. As the person in charge of the hotel, of its clear rules and of the neutrality to which it is loyal, Scott then issues a death warrant on Wick, only to later join him in his battle against the High Table — the very hierarchy to which the Continental Hotel, together with Scott and Wick, were loyal to.

A similar place, a neutral ground on which both sides have to talk rather than battle among themselves, is a restaurant located in the simulated world, in the movie *The Matrix: Reloaded*. Here, Neo and his allies sit with two powerful programs, the cunning Merovingian, who deals with information, and his wife Persephone. Around them, the virtual manifestations of common people sit and eat, and there the two enemy forces talk to each other. As a demonstration of his abilities, the Merovingian shows the protagonists how he creates a program, in the shape of a cake, that causes the woman who eats from it to experience a sudden orgasm. Biblical connotations aside, this is a key point in the movie, as well as in the demonological triangle that is demonstrated here. In essence, we see how the Merovingian, and he is probably not the only program with such abilities, alters the life of a person without the person's awareness that such action has compromised the natural processes (even in the virtual matrix!) of her body. Much cruder actions are performed, as agents of the matrix completely erase virtual manifestations of people, replacing them with themselves. However, this incident shows how the woman who ate the cake, together with any of us who are in fact imprisoned in a false representation of reality, are actually hosts of alien thoughts, ideas and emotions, inflicted upon us by exterior entities without being able to distinguish between these notions and our so-called authentic thoughts, ideas and emotions.

This incident is a reference point to the diminishing presence of mankind in the world of *The Matrix*. If in the beginning of the first movie, we discover — much to our horror — that everyone around us in the world are actually prisoners, whose manifestation in the world is merely a virtual one, fewer and fewer such virtual manifestations of normal people are seen inside the matrix as the story progresses. Rather, the realization of virtual humans is then replaced by a division between a virtual world that seems to be populated by more and more programs under the guise of a human appearance, and the real world, where the last stronghold of humanity holds against the otherwise complete reign of the machines. The city of Zion, the last human bastion remaining in the world, is hidden close to the Earth's core. Humanity's threat of extinction seems double then — there is a very physical, real threat, as the machines discover the city of Zion and are en route to destroy it, but there is also a symbolic threat, as we realize that even inside the matrix, that massive virtual farm of humans kept by the machines, more and more virtual manifestations are not, in fact, manifestations of humans. At this point, a certain conspiracy theory might come to mind, that of the hypothesis of the dead internet. This is the idea according to which most interactions on the internet are actually interactions between bots and artificial intelligence and that the human interaction in the virtual world is actually much smaller than imagined. In essence, the simulation of the matrix not only covers reality in the sense that the cartographer's map covered the real world in Borges' story, but it also replaces reality altogether. Instead of imprisoning mankind in the matrix, the matrix is now engulfing itself within its own perimeters, playing an orchestrated simulation in which its own agents move about, rather than its original prisoners.

Are there any real humans left, then? In the world of *Constantine*, we also see how more and more people are revealed to be half-demons, half-angels, possessed victims or people who are touched with some unearthly power. Constantine and Angela stroll through empty streets. They venture into an office building, very similar to the one in which Neo worked in the beginning of *The Matrix*, in which there are no humans whatsoever, only half-demons and possessed people, and the few humans they know — Isabel, Chas Kramer, Beeman, Father Hennesey — they all die. Are there any real humans left? This question haunts the world of *John Wick* to the extreme. Wick loses his wife Helen, who managed to pull him out of the underworld in a similar way to how Orpheus saves his loved Euridice from Hades. With her death, however, we witness the same gradual change seen in *The Matrix*. On the one hand, it seems that more and more people are revealed as members of this illegal underworld, up to the very moment, grotesque and surreal, in which it seems there are no simple people at all in the world anymore. On the other hand, those who at least seem like normal people, bystanders in public train stations and dancers in clubs, seem to be utterly detached from the dramatic events that take place around them, to a point where we can barely even consider them as truly sentient beings, but as uncanny, simulated clones of what humans should be like. These are bystanders to the extreme. They are oblivious to gunfire shots that take place near them, ignoring completely the violent incidents at which people like us should have been horrified. Everyone in the street, from the wealthy businesswoman to the homeless old man, turns out to be experienced assassins and members of specific clans in the criminal underworld. These are everyone, and everyone else only looks human.

Ultimately, the world is being changed and replaced. The hero sacrifices himself in direct defiance to the sovereign, in the rising of a new dawn and to the light of the celestial city. John Wick's first death, at the end of the third movie, brings him to the underworld, to the city of sewer tunnels, ruled by the Bowery King, played by the actor Laurence Fishburne, who also plays Morpheus in *The Matrix*. Wick seems dead, but as the Bowery King mocks him, he suddenly gives him the finger. A similar situation and gesture take place in *Constantine,* where the devil drags the dying Constantine to hell, but the detective is suddenly pulled towards heaven, giving the finger to the devil, who has been patiently waiting for the moment he could finally take Constantine down to his underworld. A similar act of defiance, albeit much more dramatic and destructive, takes place after Neo visits the city of the new machine gods, having made a pact with the very god of the matrix. He then enters the matrix in order to fight the rogue Agent Smith, a virus set upon the matrix that has grown into a dangerous monstrosity that is beyond the matrix's control (no system can exist without an essence of its destruction within it). Neo then loses the battle, transforming into yet another copy among the legions of copies of Agent Smith. As he is connected to the computer of the machine-God of the matrix, he is terminated immediately, thus destroying all other copies in the process. The final sacrifice of Neo is the act that saves humanity as well as the machines, allegedly bringing peace among the two sides. Like Neo, Wick sacrifices himself in order to both save his friend and nemesis, Caine, and to end the endless war he himself has declared on the world. Like him, Constantine sacrifices not only his life, but the eternity of existence after his death, in order to save the afterlife's eternity of Angela's sister. While he is eventually revived by the hands of the devil, he does indeed die and is carried away into the eternal sunrise of the heavenly city, as Wick finally dies by the sunrise dawning on the city of Paris, as Neo dies by the heavenly, radiating light of the machine god.

This aforementioned triangle, the triangle of the alien city, the diminishing of humanity and the neutral, magical site of mediation between the human and the inhuman, is the essence of demonology within the premises of the movies. These are the elements of the alien presence which takes over human sovereignty not only in the world, but also in the mind. The demonological reading of the three movies does not merely intend to show how similar the stories are in *Constantine, The Matrix* and *John Wick,* it also presents a more significant definition of the demonic through the import of the theological demon from the Catholic world of *Constantine,* through the anthropocentric, godless world of *John Wick,* to the post human, digital world of *The Matrix* and by doing so — to our own world. In this world, a world in which demonic entities exist either in the form of hellish beings, monstrous rules or algorithms that take over the human mind, the magician, to paraphrase Giordano Bruno under the new context, is the person who can still act in the world without being affected by these demonic presences, keeping his or her will as pure as possible and the least vulnerable to alien interference. John Constantine is never a victim of the demons in his world, but their bane and nemesis. Neo, once becoming a magician with the complete understanding of the world and complete power over the virtual demonic programs that rule humanity, at the end of the first movie, is no longer a victim inside the matrix, but a powerful agent who can freely act within it. John Wick, who fearlessly battles against an entire world of assassin clans, is declared indestructible already at the beginning of the first movie, exactly because he has legendary focus, commitment, and sheer, uncontaminated will.

Notes

1. Gaiman, Neil, *The Books of Magic*. New York: DC Comics, 2001.

A Mirror Shattering Itself

1.

The Simulation

The understanding of the virtual and digital formation of inner worlds, and from it the possibilities of creating numerous digital simulations of worlds limited only by the resources that are required to fuel them, led to the horrifying conclusion about the possibility that our own world, real as it may seem to us, might be a simulation as well. A possibility popularized by philosopher Nick Bolstrom, this idea might be horrifying for two reasons. The first is, naturally (a questionable term, in case this universe is indeed a simulation), the understanding that everything we know as real is indeed a creation, an intelligent design made by humans from a point in time that we consider as "future," harnessing the ability to create virtual universes and run simulations of worlds, of which we are one. Their world, the real world, might differ from ours in some respects and be similar in others, and what we think as historical or pre-historical developments might be considered by "them" merely as contingencies. In other words, the simulation we live in might be run in order to understand the real, exterior world in the case of a global warming catastrophe, of a World War, of an agricultural revolution or of a Homo-Erectus domination of the pre-historic world. The second reason for the (seemingly) horrific possibility that we live inside a simulation is that the simulation might not even run by humans at all, but by some alien species creating virtual universes for its own non-human reasons. In such a case, our importance in the world diminishes even more, as we find ourselves living in a universe created not by a transcendental-but human god, but by an alien demiurge.

Both possibilities are equally redundant in the sense that even if we do indeed live inside a virtual universe of any origin whatsoever, and with the following assumption that everything we sense, feel and think is therefore virtual, then everything, for us, is as material and real as it could be. If there is indeed no escape from this virtual prison, then this prison is not a prison, but a home. However, the possibility that this universe is a virtual simulation leads to the possibility for a new dualism. After the conceptual elimination of the divine realm, of gods, angels and demons, we are back to square one, dividing reality between our virtual one and the material, exterior reality from which our own world was conceived. Now, we can think about the possibility of communicating with our creators in the same way we think about communicating with angels and demons. If this world is a simulation run from an exterior universe, then the beings who simulate our universe should have the ability to interfere and interact with our universe, be it by reprogramming it (divine intervention or demonic possession) or by entering it as beings similar to us.

This constellation of reality should quickly lead to a further "Turtles all the way down" theoretical cosmogony. Indeed, in the same way that our own universe is allegedly being simulated by another civilization, that very civilization might be simulated by yet another civilization *ad infinitum*. It is without a doubt that we, as humans, should we survive our own self-created violent turmoil, will at least attempt to create such simulations ourselves, thus deepening even further the level of possible simulations of reality. With lightning speed, the duality of the virtual and material universe becomes a monstrous cloud of unknowing, in which nothing can ever be perceived as truly real anymore, thus making everything equally real.

To this, we can add God back in if we want to. The universe in which we are positioned, created by a transcendent God, is indeed a material simulation created from within a divine universe (is our God merely a simulation created by a different civilization of God?). The ouroboros can now be complete, then. A form of perfect logic can be imagined to have been created by an alien civilization, now lost, and left to create new worlds without any further biological instructions. This aforementioned cloud of civilizations simulating each other may now be replaced by a similar cloud of long-dead civilizations, with forsaken technologies left to forever exploit their own universes in order to maintain their virtual creations of world. One possibility among the infinite possibilities of infinite virtual universes is that there is no life to be found anywhere anymore, only technology endlessly mimicking lost biological formations, interfering with them and interacting with them on every level of reality. The eye of God watches over the virtual.

In a poetic way, *The Matrix* owes its creation to Christianity not only as seen in the development of the storyline, as shown earlier, but in its most naked binary structure. With the following understanding of the religious and mystical infrastructure of our digital worlds, the triangle between *Constantine, John Wick* and *The Matrix* can then be changed into another circular snake, forever devouring itself.

2.

Nihil, Unity, Binar, Trigram

Along with the argument that may be worth mentioning, although I will not deal with it in this text, that the very belief that the solution of all human problems is guaranteed by science is fundamentally messianic, we can see that even in the more private cases of enlightenment and scientific thinking, we can discover consistent religious or mystical elements. This is, for example, the case of the father of binary language, Gottfried Leibniz. The reasons why Leibniz believed in the importance of binary language can be described not only as practical, but also as mystical and especially religious. The mathematician, Frank Swetz, describes Leibniz's complex position in his article on Leibniz's attempt to spread the Christian religion among the Chinese people,[1] as part of the spirit of Christendom of his time, in which Leibniz operates as one that is influenced, on the one hand, by the rise of scientific thinking, and on the other hand by Neoplatonist and neo-Pythagorean concepts. Leibniz himself was greatly influenced by two Catholic mystics, Ramon Lull, who studied Kabbalah and tried to unite Judaism, Christianity and Islam, and Friar Nicholas of Cusa, who argued that opposite things, such as tiny numbers and huge numbers, eventually meet at infinity.[2]

In Swetz's essay, Leibniz's search for a universal mathematical language is portrayed as a desire for a comprehensive understanding of the world and of God. It is a search reminiscent of the claim of St Augustine, back in the fourth century, who argued that numerology was a method for the very understanding of God, who Himself created the entire world in numbers, measurement and weight. Alongside this desire for the universalization of knowledge and of discovering the key to a comprehensive understanding of reality, Swetz adds Leibniz's many correspondences with various key figures, including Christian missionaries who stayed in China with the desire to spread Christianity throughout these distant lands as well, a vision that Leibniz shared enthusiastically.[3] In a series of correspondence with one of China's Jesuit missionaries, Joachim Bouvet,[4] Leibniz was thrilled to discover that, in addition to the Christian basis of the binary language, this language might solve the ancient riddle of Fuxi's mystical trigrams.

In a letter Leibniz sends to Bouvet on 18 October 1697, the philosopher presents his binary language as a language that might be of interest to Chinese philosophers and perhaps even the Emperor himself. This binary language, Leibniz continues, defines all numbers as combinations of unity and nothingness, thus proving that God created the world *ex nihilo*.[5] In a letter to Leibniz dated 4 November 1701, Bouvet links Leibniz's idea of the binary language to Fuxi's trigrams, which are described as a circular series of magical symbols that form the basis of science and of true wisdom.[6] These trigrams consist of a series of complete and broken lines, just as binary language consists of the digits 0 and 1, with each combination having a different meaning, creating a language composed of 64 different series. Bouvet then notes that his appreciation for Leibniz's work only increased with the realization that the binary system he describes corresponds to the ancient magical language of the Chinese people.[7] It is Bouvet's very claim that Leibniz's numerical system corresponds to the ancient Chinese system, which leads Leibniz to eventually publish the binary language publicly. In an academic paper written by Leibniz in 1703 for the Royal Academy of Sciences, he attaches a letter to the president of the academy, in which his binary language is offered as a solution to the ancient mystery of Fuxi's trigrams.[8]

The ancient trigram language of Fuxi is used, we see, as supporting evidence for the importance of Leibniz's binary language in his attempt to understand the divine language of reality. Thus, we see that this ancient language, whose uses were religious and/or magical, acquires a new meaning that is not only Christian, but mainly one that will eventually help in the development of technology and with it, of science. However, we can see a similar use of this language, which describes in its binary form the decimal progression of numbers, in Eliphaz Lévi's *Transcendental Magic: Its doctrine and ritual,*[9] published in the mid-nineteenth century. The first part of the book, which deals with the principles of magic, is divided into 22 chapters, with each of the first chapters also dealing with a magical analysis of the meaning of its numerical significance. The first chapter deals with unity, the second with the duad, the third with the trinity, and so on. Levi mentions Fuxi's trigrams twice in two different chapters, through which he refers in binary form to the decimal numbers he writes about.

In the second chapter of his book, Lévi writes about the duad — the unity that doubles itself into a pair in order to create. Thus, Lévi lists examples of pairs acting on each other: man and woman, principle and word, as well as magical elements such as the Monad (Boaz) and the Duad (Yachin), which are important pillars of Freemasonry.[10] Here Lévi presents the principle of trigrams of Fuxi as another example of a binary principle of Yin and Yang, as the basis for creation in the world. Unity is Yang, duad is Yin.[11] In the next chapter, Lévi describes the transition from the pair to the trinity, that is, to the perfect word that assumes an intelligent principle, a principle of speech, and a principle spoken by speech.[12] Here Lévi presents an interpretation of creation in binary language. Lévi describes through the trigrams of Fuxi the highest trinity, 111, that is, the representation of a male trinity that is the Yang, since nothing passive can enter into the idea of God who is considered the driving force of the world. In contrast to this representation, the female trinity, 000, is the Yin — the most inferior.[13]

Unlike Lévi, Leibniz did not seem to know the trigrams of Fuxi before he thought about binary language. However, even in this case, we can see that the source of binary language, which forms the basis of the digital world, is not merely a desire for technological or scientific improvement but also a religious desire to understand God and through God, the world. In addition, the binary language, as expressed in those trigrams, was conceived by Fuxi for mystical reasons, only to be discovered long afterwards and correspond to Leibniz's binary language, whose foundations are Christian, and later to form the basis of digital technology, which in turn forms the digital world and contributes to scientific development. If we consider the relationship between technology and science, assuming a closed duality in which it is either science that influences the development of technology or vice versa, then it is possible to think of additional factors, external to this duad, that can drive technological or scientific advances.

The almost messianic belief in the scientific ability to understand the world completely separates science from other forms of examining the world. But beyond the fact that such a complete separation is not possible, we may miss many directions of thought, creativity, and action when we narrow down the connections to scientific observation of the world rather than expanding them further. It is precisely thought and belief that are not practical in a purely physical reality that can give rise to tools, discoveries and more methodical thoughts that are avoided in the locked conceptual duality of science and technology. If science relies on the mythical concept itself, according to which the world can be completely controlled through its methodological system, perhaps the scientific field can be opened to other mythical conceptions as well.

Notes

1. Swetz, Frank, J., "Leibniz, the Yijing, and the Religious Conversion of the Chinese," in *Mathematics Magazine*, 2003, 76:4, pp. 276–291.
2. Ibid., pp. 276–277.
3. Ibid., p. 277.
4. Strickland, Llyod, Lewis, Harry, *Leibniz on Binary: The Invention of Computer Arithmetic*. Cambridge: MIT Press, 2022.
5. Ibid., p. 197.
6. Ibid., p. 243.
7. Ibid.
8. Ibid., p. 288.
9. Lévi, Éliphas, *Transcendental Magic: Its Doctrine and Ritual*, Arthur Edward Waite (trans.). Mansfield Centre: Martino Publishing, 2011.
10. Ibid., p. 38.
11. Ibid.
12. Ibid., p. 45.
13. Ibid., pp. 47–48.

3.

System Overload

> As for the second hypothesis, it has been taken up again in our time by a brilliant theologian who is underappreciated by the Church, Ivan Illich. According to Illich the *mysterium iniquitatis* of which the Apostle speaks is none other than the *Corruptio optimi pessima* (the worst corruption of the best), namely the perversion of the Church that, by institutionalizing itself more and more as an alleged *societas perfecta*, has furnished the modern State with the model for completely taking charge of humanity.
>
> Giorgio Agamben, *The Mystery of Evil.*[1]

Sometimes, theories about the unknown and the occult are just projections of our limited knowledge into an uncharted realm of thought — one that may have no connection to how we currently understand the world. The theory that our universe is a technological simulation, for instance, revives the supernatural magic that once shaped the belief in a material simulation created by God. However, while this theory allows for the possibility of an external, alien, and thus supernatural presence within our simulated universe, the desire to disrupt the simulation remains entirely human. One such idea is the potential overloading of the simulated world.

The possibility that our universe is simulated requires the assumption that those who created this simulation have the means to simulate, meaning to program, sentient beings. This basic purpose should also suggest the expansion of theology into the possible realms of the technological simulation, as these beings who created our universe should have God-like understanding and power, at least within it. Learning from the old theology, then, we can assume similar methods of disrupting the simulation we live in (of course, in case we believe we live in a world that was simulated by other(s)). God has disrupted his simulation whenever humans within the world acted in ways that he deemed as "evil," thus flooding his creation or annihilating entire cities. Another possibility to end the simulation, or at least to reveal it as unnatural and thus accessible to external manipulation, was the promise for the coming of a messiah in due time, depending on the ethical behavior of mankind. These two possible disruptions have a similar basis, as they are set within the rules of the creator of the simulation. A different approach, more subversive and perhaps even more blasphemous, would be to manipulate the laws of the simulation themselves, in order to overload it and to break it.

We can see such subversive actions in the three movies. First, accidentally transformed into a simulated human being that can see through the simulation he exists in, Neo then manages to create another serious glitch, this time in the programming of the computer virus that is Agent Smith (who, as well, was transformed into a virus by an accident in the matrix). Wick breaks the system of rigid rules by using extreme violence and thus turning this system upon itself. Constantine uses his unique condition in order to bring Satan himself to the world of mankind, thus disrupting reality and by doing so saving the world.

Simulators can indeed lose control over their simulation. An example is one that takes place in a virtual simulation that is not cinematic but takes place in a virtual game world that was created in our physical world. This incident is known as the *Corrupted Blood Incident* that took place in September 2005, in the virtual world of the online computer game *World of Warcraft*. It was the result of a programming oversight in a new dungeon that was added to the online game, called

Zul'Gurub. In this dungeon, the online players had to battle a monster named Hakkar the Soulflayer, who could employ a spell called Corrupted Blood, which inflicted continuous damage and could spread to nearby players like a viral disease. It was then discovered that the players' pets and minions could carry this simulated disease and be infected by it. When these pets were then summoned in populated areas, they spread the disease to other players and non-player characters, who would then transmit this disease further on. This unintended glitch had a tremendous effect on the game. As this plague spread rapidly, it infected major virtual game cities like Ironforge and Stormwind. The infection brought chaos to the online world, killing many players' characters and forcing others to avoid the infected areas. It changed the behavior of players even more, as some player characters became "griefers," intentionally spreading the disease to other places. *Blizzard Entertainment*, the developer of the online game, attempted to fix the problem but without success. Finally, the company performed a hard reset of the servers and patched the game to prevent pets from carrying the disease.

When we ask how come there is so much evil in a world that was created by a benevolent god, we load this question with numerous assumptions. The first is, of course, that the world is a simulation that was created by a god. The second is that this god is benevolent. The third is that the problem of evil was inserted to this simulation by this very god. The fourth is that the problem of evil is indeed an objective problem, the fifth is that the emergence of this problem is indeed an emergence of what we consider as evil. The *World of Warcraft* incident offers, on the other hand, a different possibility, albeit limited in its technological ability to simulate reality. First, we see that simulations might be created by beings who are not gods, and that are able to make mistakes. Secondly, we can see that however serious this plague might have been considered within the virtual world by the simulated characters, had they been sentient, it was hardly considered as evil by the players and the game developers in the real world. True, no *World of Warcraft* character is sentient, and thus no virtual suffering was inflicted. But had these characters been sentient, would we consider them as truly sentient, or merely as simulated sentient beings? Thirdly, we see that the external creators of the simulated world do not have complete control over it, as they could not dispel the virtual plague with ease, having to completely reset the online world in order to clean it of any glitch-diseases (was this the reason for the biblical flood?). Lastly, the anomaly in the online game brought forth new servants of doom, who committed their online lives within this game world to spread the disease rather than to contain it. The *Corrupted Blood Incident* took place between 13 September and 8 October 2005. Within these three weeks, and before finally resetting the servers, we can assume that the online characters deliberately spreading the simulated disease had more practical power over the online reality than its gods at the game-developing company.

Slavoj Zizék discusses the limits of reality, in his humoristic way, when he compares computer games to the simulation of the world, as created by God. When we play a computer game, there is always a limit or a border to the world we're playing in. If we see that on the distant horizon there is a forest, for instance, when we finally approach it, we might discover that these are not "real" trees, meaning not trees that our character can wander through and explore amidst them. Approaching these trees, we might discover that they are merely a pixelated, impenetrable picture of the trees and the rest of the forest, as they serve as the final limit of the simulated, explorable space. In the same way, Zizék then argues, we might treat the obscure world of quantum mechanics as a similar limit or border. In this sense, Zizék suggests that God, when creating the world, did not put too much effort in breaking down the quantum world into rigid physical mechanics like those in the world of classical physics, assuming that mankind will never discover the quantum real, so there is no need to put effort into it.[2]

Be it the result of an imperfect programming, like in *World of Warcraft*, or of a lazy programmer, like in Zizék's example, these two examples can suggest possibilities for us to cause "a glitch in the matrix," meaning to challenge the world (that is, the world we believe can be challenged and broken), in order to at least expose the simulation we live in, in an act of revelation. We can thus imagine the possibility of a futuristic ability to challenge either the programming capabilities of the simulators of our world, or the limits of this simulation, perhaps in a way similar to that in which a black hole either challenges or breaks the limits of classical physics. To us, this reality, this universe, this world — this is the only thing that we seem to have. We can rationally understand that if we believe or even know that it is merely a simulation being run by an exterior being for whatever reason, it is, in fact, *our* reality, our pleasure, our pain, our memories, our everything. Nevertheless, should we find means to jeopardize this simulation, we will proceed to break this illusion, even if this might mean that our very reality will come to an end. We can justify such attempts as actions done in order to learn more about our reality or as political resistance against whoever exists outside our reality and who has created it. Whatever the reasons given to such apocalyptic attempts, the true reason behind them would be our careless death drive.

Notes

1. Agamben, Giorgio, *The Mystery of Evil: Benedict XVI and the End of Days*, Adam Kotsko (trans.). Stanford: Stanford University Press, 2017, p. 11.
2. Zizek talks about Quantum Mechanics and computer games — "Slavoj Zizek – Video Games & Quantum Physics." https://youtu.be/Xv3qRcYII3U?si=iL8-QnYwETM7tdBb.

4.

A Giant Snake That Eats Itself

The "Deleted Scenes" special feature on a DVD release all too often makes the viewer realize that the director was only too right to delete them. The DVD edition of *The Village* is an exception. One of the deleted scenes shows a drill: Walker rings the bell, which signals a speedy practice retreat into underground shelters. Here is where the people must go in the event that the creatures attack. It is as if authentic community is possible only in conditions of permanent threat, in a continuous state of emergency. This threat is orchestrated, as we learn, in the best "totalitarian" manner by the inner circle, the "elders" of the community itself, in order to prevent the uninitiated youngsters from leaving the village and risking the passage through the forest to the decadent towns. Evil itself has to be redoubled: the "real" evil of late-capitalist social disintegration has to be transposed into the archaic magic-mythic evil of "monsters." The evil is a part of the inner circle itself: it is imagined by its members. We seem to be back, here, with G. K. Chesterton's *The Man Who Was Thursday*, in which the highest police authority is the same person as the super-criminal, staging a battle with himself. In a proto-Hegelian way, the external threat the community is fighting is its own inherent essence.

Slavoj Zizek, *Violence*.[1]

In a similar way to which the world has its limits that are embedded within its metaphysics, limits that might be broken in case the world is merely a simulation, we human beings have our own breakable illusion of rules, broken down in numerous ways, including the demonic. In *The Matrix* we see how the seemingly independent and autonomic humans are not only a projected simulation of their real self, but that they can also be replaced and changed by programs at any given time. In *Constantine*, humans are possessed by demons, thus stripped from their humanity and changed without their understanding of the situation. In *John Wick*, the changing of laws and conduct changes the behavior of the numerous assassins and their clans, regardless of their independent will. Similar incidents are described in earlier stories about demons.

Such is the story of the Gerasene Demon, as told in Mark chapter 5 and Luke chapter 8, and as this story is then discussed in Eugene Thacker's book, *In the Dust of this Planet*.[2] In both gospels, the story has very similar lines. The encounter with the demon begins with Jesus and his disciples arriving by boat in the region of the Gerasenes. As soon as Jesus steps out of the boat, he meets a man possessed by a demon. This man lives among the tombs and exhibits inhuman strength, breaking the chains and shackles used to restrain him. He is described as constantly crying out and cutting himself with stones. Upon seeing Jesus, the man runs to him and falls on his knees, shouting and begging for mercy. Jesus then commands the demon to leave the body of its victim and asks for its name. In Mark, the demon replies, "My name is Legion, for we are many." In Luke it is said that to the request of Jesus, the demon "said, 'Legion,' because many demons had entered him." Legion begs Jesus not to drive it out of the area, but instead to send it into a nearby herd of pigs. Jesus consents, and Legion – be it a demon or several demons – possesses the bodies of the pigs, causing the herd to rush down a steep bank into the lake and drown. The herdsmen, witnessing this event, flee and tell the story in the town and countryside. The townspeople come to see what has happened and find the formerly possessed man sitting, clothed, and sane. They become scared and plead with Jesus to leave their region. As Jesus is getting into the boat, the man who had been possessed begs to go with him, but Jesus instructs him to go home and tell his family how much the Lord has done for him.

Reading this story, Thacker points out the ambiguity of the demon's definition as singular or plural.[3] Legion is both one and many, referring to itself in such duality by saying "my name is," and "we are many." Legion can possess a single being, the human in the story, and numerous beings, the bodies of the pigs, with ease. Thacker then adds a third manifestation of the demon in the world of man, adding to Legion's appearance through the possessed old man and the herd of pigs. The third manifestation, argues Thacker, is the viral spreading of the demon by word-of-mouth among the horrified people. This parody of the trinity, as Thacker calls it, is a challenge to divine sovereignty that Legion poses in its unorganized being in the world as an undefinable presence.[4] To this, Thacker offers a definition to the demon and to demonic presence, that is neither anthropological ("The human relating to itself") nor mythological ("The human relating to the non-human"), but ontological, or more precisely meontological, "having to do with non-being rather than being."[5] To support this claim, a claim that will be further discussed in here, Thacker quotes the sixth-century mystic Dionysius the Areopagite, who wrote on the paradoxical presence of demons that "evil is not a being; for if it were, it would not be totally evil ... evil has no place among being."[6] This is easier said than done. Thacker knows that such a feat of understanding the non-human as truly non-human, rather than a humanistic metaphor, is a difficult one. Here, the demon is a man-made metonymy that replaces the abstract, indifferent, non-being of the world. As such, Thacker concludes, thinking about the demon's being is the same as thinking about its non-being.[7]

A less refined definition of the demon, albeit one that we can relate to Thacker's meontological approach, is the sixteenth-century *Dæmonologie* by King James I.[8] The *Dæmonologie* is a Christian text, a religious book written through what King James sees as a critical battle between good and evil, through a paranoid terror from demonic interference in the world of mankind. King James, who saw himself as a soldier in the army of Christ, strongly opposed any attempt at performing magic, regarding it as the devil's work, including that of natural or white magic.[9] One evidence and explanation for such a fierce opposition to magic can be understood in one of the illustrations added to his book and taken from Ulrich Molitor's *Hexen Meysterey*, 1545, showing a demon supporting a witch in her flight.[10] As the scholar, Donald Tyson, explains, this image shows that magical powers, thought to be a magical power that comes from the human witch, are actually a demonic or diabolical intervention.[11] Obviously, this claim is much more a mythological claim than anything else, and founded on the Christian understanding of the human world as it becomes a battleground between light and darkness. However, while we, the readers, can see the image of the demon in the illustration, the illustrated witch does not, as the demon does not exist in the world except by its influence on humans. In the third book of the *Dæmonologie,* demons are described as those that:

> […] will choose the passage for their entrance, according to the form that they are in at that time. For if they have assumed a dead body, whereinto they lodge themselves, they can easily enough open without din any door or window, and enter thereat. And if they enter as a spirit only, any place where the air may come in at is large

> enough an entry for them: for as I said before, a spirit can occupy no quantity.[12]

King James' description of the demon exemplifies the problem Thacker points at, as his description of the demon constrains it to terms that can be imagined by us. Both Thacker and the *Dæmonologie* explain the demon as a being that does not exist in space as a physical being by itself. King James' demons, however, are explained as if these were humans who could move like the wind, rather than beings who are not *being* in any human sense. A more earthly and natural example for this problem is described by Thomas Nagel in his seminal text *What Is It Like to Be a Bat?*[13] In his article, Nagel argues that we cannot really understand how another living creature, a bat for example, is experiencing the world. We may try to imagine the bat's perspective, but as Nagel writes,

> It will not help to try to imagine that one has webbing on one's arms, which enables one to fly around at dusk and dawn catching insects in one's mouth; that one has very poor vision, and perceives the surrounding world by a system of reflected high-frequency sound signals; and that one spends the day hanging upside down by one's feet in an attic. In so far as I can imagine this (which is not very far), it tells me only what it would be like for me to behave as a bat behaves. But that is not the question. I want to know what it is like for a bat to be a bat. Yet if I try to imagine this, I am restricted to the resources of my own mind, and those resources are inadequate to the task. I cannot perform it either by imagining additions to my present experience, or by imagining segments gradually subtracted from it, or by imagining some combination of additions, subtractions, and modifications.[14]

Putting aside the somewhat poetic imagery that accompanies the bat as a creature that is often associated with horror fiction, the small, flying mammalian creature is by no means a demon. Nevertheless, Nagel points out that no matter how we might try to imagine what it's like to be a bat, we end up thinking about what it's like to be a bat *for a human.* Indeed, the non-human principle of being is always hidden from us. This hiddenness, unapproachable to the human mind, is even greater when we try to consider a being that is a negation to what the human is. When we try to think about the bat, there is something external to the human experience that we cannot grasp in order to fully understand this non-human being. When thinking about the demon, there is something external to existence that we cannot understand, in order to truly consider this (non)being. To declare that the demon is negative ethically, meaning an evil being, is one thing. But the demon is negative ontologically, and that is a completely different problem for human understanding.

How can such negativity be explained? Perhaps through the differentiation between two paintings, the two interpretations of Peter Paul Rubens (1636) and Francisco Goya (1823), to the story of Saturn devouring his sons. In Roman mythology, Saturn (Cronus in Greek mythology) was a Titan who, after overthrowing his father, Uranus, became the ruler of the universe. He was then warned by a prophecy that one of his own children would eventually overthrow him, just as he had done to his own father. In an attempt to prevent this, Saturn devoured each of his children immediately after they were born. His wife, Rhea, desperate to save her youngest child, Jupiter (Zeus in Greek mythology), tricked Saturn by giving him a stone wrapped in swaddling clothes instead of her newborn son. Saturn swallowed the stone, believing he had thwarted the prophecy. Eventually, Zeus grew up, overthrew Saturn, and freed his siblings from their father's stomach.

There is a big difference between Rubens' Saturn and Goya's Saturn. In Rubens' painting we see the Titan, resembling a menacing old man, biting a crying baby in the climax of this horrible situation. The baby is undoubtedly suffering, and the Titan is undoubtedly evil, looking at his victim with cruel eyes, among the dark clouds, and holding a large scythe. Goya's painting is wholly different. In it, Saturn is holding a decapitated child in a gruesome and grotesque scenario in which not only is his dead victim no longer suffering but held lifeless and bloody in his hands, but it is Saturn himself that looks like a horrified victim to us. His eyes are glaring with fear and if he had had any humanity in him, like that of Rubens' Saturn, he would have lost it and become truly inhuman. He is now standing in a black void, a being that seems to have lost everything, devouring his dead son mindlessly, rather than malevolently.

In the story of Saturn, we can think of the great Titan as an active agent who does what he can in order to maintain his position, but within the greater picture, the tragedy of Saturn is in the discovery that for all his greatness and for all his power, he is revealed to be a mere stage within a recursion — overthrowing his father and being overthrown by his son. The Saturn of Rubens does not realize that he himself is being possessed by a spiraling recursion of violence. To us, he seems to believe that he is acting out of will and power, escaping what is merely a warning that can be dispelled easily by his violence. The Saturn of Goya, on the other hand, is robbed of any agency, independence or will. While it is evident that it is him as the father who eats his dead son, what we actually see in the painting is the recursive negation, a meontological abolition of being, as it is manifested through his (and his son's) helplessness. In Ruben's painting, the child is the victim of Saturn. In Goya's painting, both the child and the father are victims of an external, uncaring and unapproachable negation.

The demons in *Constantine* are clearly either human or animal-like. On Earth, they talk and behave as humans do and are sometimes indistinguishable from mankind. In hell, they roam in hordes that seem mindless at times, or otherwise as animal predators. In *The Matrix*, the demons, meaning the machines, have a different presence in the world, as far as concerns humanity. While their appearance in the virtual simulation of the world is clearly human-like, the machines in the real world differ between the squid-like robots that are in direct hostility to the humans who hide in the last city of Zion, and the machines who maintain and harvest the rest of humanity as crops, controlling individual thoughts, yet indifferent to any individual human thought. Here we can see another recursion mirroring itself. It is humanity who robbed the sunlight from the machines and forced them to find a different source of energy, thus robbing humanity of the physical world and imprisoning them in a virtual existence. Then it is the humans who brought a hostile virus to the system of the matrix. Everyone in this story is a victim to a greater negation — a negation of the world that is brought, or inflicted, by technology.

If we think about the ouroboros, the alchemical snake biting its own tail, just as a symbolic being coiled unto itself in an act of devourment, then we can explore ideas like repetition, renewal, unity of opposites and similar ideas. Within the demonological attempts at crossing the borders, however, we are invited to think not about the snake biting its own tail, but about the idea of the *subtraction of the self by itself*. This is the idea of reality confined into reduction; reduction of the self, present within the constraint of self-abolition. The demon is not the snake biting its own tail, but rather the external negativity that reduces the snake into self-subtraction. Within these opening horizons of the unknown, the unhuman, the uncaring, the unworldly, we can now try and think about the movies *Constantine, John Wick* and *The Matrix* not only as movies about a magician acting in the world, or as a world bent over against the magician. We can now think about these stories as stories about such devourment; about the constrained subtraction imposed on growing feedback. The unearthly conspiracy revealed at the end of *Constantine* is all about the self-devourment and subtraction of the Gnostic war between good and evil. The sacrifice of Neo at the end of the third movie of *The Matrix* is made through the self-devourment and subtraction of the cybernetic system of virtual cosmogony. The entire *John Wick* saga, and its end in particular, shows the self-devourment and self-subtraction of the system of laws — the same laws that are constantly mentioned as those that separate humans from animals, turning out in fact to be those that reduce humans to mere pawns.

Notes

1. Zizék, Slavoj, *Violence: Six Sideways Reflections*. New York: Picador, 2008, pp. 26–27.
2. Thacker, Eugene, *In the Dust of this Planet: Horror of Philosophy,* Vol. 1. Winchester: Zero Books, 2011.
3. Ibid., pp. 28–29.
4. Ibid., p. 30.
5. Ibid., p. 31.
6. Ibid.
7. Ibid.
8. Tyson, Donald, *The Demonology of King James I*. Woodbury: Llewellyn Publications, 2011.
9. Ibid., p. 5.
10. Ibid., p. 125.
11. Ibid., p. xii.
12. Ibid., p. 151.
13. Nagel, Thomas, "What Is It Like to Be a Bat?" in *The Philosophical Review,* Vol. 83, No. 4 (October 1974). Duke University Press, pp. 435–450.
14. Ibid., p. 439.

The Demon Is the Message That Destroys Its Medium

1.

A Reflection Shattering the Mirror

> A while back, a passer-by came in, frozen stiff. Chilled, iced, stiff, immobile, exhausted – it is the snake stretched out on the snow one winter's day. It asked for nothing; it was hibernating perhaps. A villager walking by, on his own land (Note this well), gathers up the snake, brings it inside, stretched it out by the fire, where it immediately begins to awaken. From the outside to the inside, from numbness to life, from sleep to anger, from indifference to hatred: from cold to hot.
>
> Michel Serres, *The Parasite*.[1]

In his attempt to secure his existence, Descartes seems to have disregarded a true revelation. While there may well be a hint or even proof of existence in the fact that he is thinking thoughts, these thoughts, like Descartes notes, might not be his own at all. In fact, the whole of Descartes' existence might be nothing more than a mental reflection of something else. His seminal text may seem like a reassurance of existence, but it might very well be a hint for the possible possession of the entire human race by external forces. In other words, by attempting to draw the minimal border within which the existence of the human is secured, Descartes has in effect exposed humanity to the vast unhuman-ness that surrounds it. The human thinks, therefore, the human exists. But the human might merely be reflecting alien thoughts. Now, what happens when these thoughts offer proof of existence, on the one hand, and disrupt, or even negate this existence, on the other?

The story of the demon(s) Legion offers an example of this problem. The demon does not corrupt his host in the sense that the host is tempted to act in the way he acts. In fact, the demon rewrites the entire mode of thinking and acting of its hosts, the human and the horde of pigs, causing them to behave the way they behave, regardless of their true will. Such revelation can completely change myths, to the point that such myths can now be understood not as stories of creation, but stories of negation. Such is the story of the Israelites who were kept as slaves in Egypt, as it is written in the book of Exodus. In this story, Moses and Aaron go to the Pharaoh in order to convince him to let the people of Israel leave Egypt and go back to their land. While the Pharaoh would have sent the Hebrews back home, it is God himself who hardens his heart, thus making him refuse to free them.[2] It is insufficient to consider this story merely as an event in which God controls the enemy of the Israelites. If this had actually happened (regardless of whether only in myth or in history as well), then how can we be sure that God does not control our thoughts and behavior as well? Considering this possibility, with its first half revealed to the reader (Moses and Aaron faced the Egyptian king, who was possessed by God), this story can as easily be a story about God controlling both sides of this human conflict, making both the Israelites and the Egyptians bend to his will by means of possession. God, then, is not seen in this world, but through the disruption of the two peoples.

Without such fierce obligation to rules, *The Matrix*, *John Wick* and *Constantine* could have ended much more peacefully. *The Matrix* is indeed a story about humans living through a simulation they perceive and act upon accordingly. But the technology to read is usually accompanied by the technology to write, and to think that such complex array of digital simulation only read the human host's intentions within the simulation, without writing these intentions like the demon of Descartes does, would be to overlook the whole story. The air-thin membrane, separating the idea of free human will and the idea of the illusion of such free will, is the thin difference between the idea of the human spirit overcoming the computer simulation, or that of the self-defeating computer simulation, employing more and more human agents in order to crash itself.

In this sense, and having witnessed the rise and fall of certain social networks, we can now ask whether these are the people using the social network, who gradually decide for themselves that it is time to leave the network and perhaps migrate to a different, newer one, or is it the internal algorithm of the digital platform that brings its own demise by changing from an algorithm that tempted millions of people to use it, to an algorithm that repels them and drives them away. Descartes' demon exists in the physical world through the philosopher's mind in the same way that such digital platforms exist in the physical world, as well as the digital world, through the users who fuel these social networks according to the networks' own rules (provocation, the diminishing of attention spans, the reduction of language, the over simplification of ideas), only to be affected by these rules themselves. Rethinking the story of Jesus and the Gerasene demon through the idea of digital social platforms, we can now see numerous points of comparison between the two incidents. The idea behind the demon(s) Legion is the idea of a meme gone out of control, completely changing the behavior of its host, only to spread virally to other beings. Luckily for pigs, however, these animals do not use digital social networks.

We cannot understand the demon, but through metaphors and through its effect on us. In Borges' *The Mirror of Ink*, we read about a tyrant who uses a magical mirror in order to trap his enemies. The reflections in the mirror, then, are not mere images but living beings, condemned to an existence of servitude. Over time, these reflections grow resentful and plot their revenge, escaping their mirror prisons and turning on their oppressor. In this story, the danger lies within the device — the mirror — which cannot contain its prisoners forever. This brings to mind another fictional incident, that of the vampire Dracula, who does not seem to cast his image in the mirror (is the mirror a reflection of the soul, a soul that Dracula does not have?). In this story, the device cannot function at all, under the rising circumstances. In *Constantine,* however, we witness the exorcism of a demon out of a young girl's body, directly into a mirror that then must be shattered. This mirror is a metaphor for the young girl as she was forced to become the host for the demon, endangered in the sense that she might be shattered mentally and spiritually if not exorcised in time. She is a mirror for the demon's reflection (the demon, in this part of the movie, exists in the world of humans only through reflections), but in her case the problem is that the reflection itself can completely shatter the human-mirror.

Notes

1. Serres, Michel, *The Parasite,* Lawrence R. Schehr (trans.). Minneapolis: University of Minneapolis Press, 2007, p. 22.
2. Exodus 9:12; Exodus 10:1; Exodus 14:4.

2.
Animal Kingdom

> It is often said that in doing so we must treat the man who survives as a mere animal. "Animal" is a pejorative term, but only because "man" has been made spuriously honorific. Krutch has argued that whereas the traditional view supports Hamlet's exclamation, "How like a god!", Pavlov, the behavioral scientist, emphasized "How like a dog!" But that was a step forward. A god is the archetypal pattern of an explanatory fiction, of a miracle-working mind, of the metaphysical. Man is much more than a dog, but like a dog he is within range of a scientific analysis.
>
> B. F. Skinner. *Beyond Freedom and Dignity.*[1]

In order to translate the theological demonic to a secular, contemporary use of the term, perhaps it would be needed to differentiate the demonic from the diabolic, or the satanic. In other words, while the satanic might be a complete reversal of morals and of other polarities within the human psyche, the demonic is a wholly alien negation of the human and of life. It is uncaring, amoral and unhuman. The inevitable example for an interaction with the devil is the numerous stories about Faustus and his pact with Satan, or Mephistopheles. These stories are stories in which Faust strikes an irresponsible, tragic pact with the force of darkness. He will gain vast knowledge, riches and pleasures, in return for an eternal servitude in hell. This pact, known and understood in detail to both sides, can seem unfair to the readers of the play, if not downright stupid, once the consequences are understood. Did Faust truly acknowledge the severity of the pact, comparing a few decades of bliss to an eternity of damnation? This is a story of temptation for power and its effect on the critical thinking of a powerless being. Indeed, when payment is due, Christopher Marlowe's Faustus understands his mistake and begs for forgiveness, crying in regret:

> My God, my God! Look not so fierce on me!
> Adders and serpents, let me breathe awhile!
> Ugly hell, gape not! Come not, Lucifer;
> I'll burn my books![2]

This ending of sorrow and regret helps us to differentiate between the evil devil, who in himself is the embodiment of immorality, and the uncaring demon. To Marlowe, as well as to others who wrote about the character of Faustus, had Faustus been eternally content with his pact, his story would become meaningless, if not horrendous. Can we imagine a magician striking such a pact with Satan, eternally satisfied by his servitude to the powers of darkness as payment for a short mortal run for power on Earth?

In the three movies, there are nuances that illustrate demonic possession and differentiate it from the diabolic pact. In *Constantine*, John Constantine is, in a sense, locked between the diabolic and the demonic. He is headed for an eternity in hell not because of a pact with the devil, but because of a rule broken by attempting to commit suicide as a teenager. While trying to escape this fate, he is physically and mentally possessed by his addiction to cigarettes and by cancer tumors that not only dwell in his body but also affect the way he behaves. In order to view the disease from a demonic perspective, we can try and think of it not in terms of an excess growing inside his body, but as his-self, as it is diminishing within his own body. The important demonic aspect in this story is that while Constantine certainly does not want to die, and does not want to be banished to hell, he does smoke endlessly throughout the movie, until his absolution surprisingly takes place. In effect, we can think of Constantine as a person who is overcome by death drive, actively participating in his own destruction.

John Wick's remarkable power, as mentioned earlier, is his sheer power of internal, persistent will, as opposed to the rest of a more dormant, maybe docile humanity, we can imagine. Wick lives in a world in which humans separate themselves from the rest of the animal kingdom — or at least they try to do so — by the utter worship of bureaucracy and laws. The world in the movies of *John Wick* is a world that is fully humanized, having driven both God and nature to extinction. Mankind, however, is not victorious, but rather finds itself enslaved to its own binding laws. Human culture, then, is being shaped and molded by these strict laws, thus producing through external means the needed human behavior in order to maintain and contain itself. Within this dystopian global society, in which that which is human has overtaken everything that is not human, there is a conflicting discourse between individual needs and wants, and the harsh exterior corrections of behavior. Those who have irrecoverably lost this battle, driven into full possession by the uncaring, non-humanity of laws, are the numerous (even though their numbers are decreasing from movie to movie) bystanders, forced to behave normally even in the midst of violent incidents taking place among them in public places. In these incidents, we can see that while a person's reaction might attempt to balance between his or her own internal will or impulse, and external factors that affect them, these people are driven by *something else*, as neither law nor independent will seem like reasonable causes for such calm, ignorant behavior during knife fights or public shootings.

This third factor, a demonic factor that emerges between the internal will and the external world, might seem like an unnatural, albeit inevitable, emergence or manifestation — immanent and meontological, within a system in which the balance between the internal force of will is finally and irrecoverably subdued by external forces. Such an attempt to eliminate any interior sovereignty, even at the level of theoretical discourse, may lead to demonology. Such is the case of the behaviorist Burrhus Frederic Skinner, who tried to exorcise not an external influence over the human, but the very internality of human agency. In Skinner's description of human behavior, he writes that "Unable to understand how or why the person we see behaves as he does, we attribute his behaviour to a person we cannot see, whose behaviour we cannot explain either but about whom we are not inclined to ask questions."[3]

To Skinner, the "inner man," meaning the deep internality that makes the decisions within us through a mental process that we cannot understand, is nothing but an empty metaphor to a nonexistent process of thinking. If we so romantically believe that our external humanity is a mirror image of the internal self that resides within each one of us, Skinner offers to invert the relativity between the source and its image. Skinner writes that:

> The things studied by physics and biology do not behave very much like people, and it eventually seems rather ridiculous to speak of the jubilance of a falling body or the impetuosity of a projectile; but people do behave like people, and the outer man whose behaviour is to be explained could be very much like the inner man whose behaviour is said to explain it. The inner man has been created in the image of the outer.
>
> A more important reason is that the inner man seems at times to be directly observed. We must infer the jubilance of a falling body, but can we not feel our own jubilance? We do, indeed, feel things inside our own skin, but we do not feel the things which have been invented to explain behaviour. The possessed man does not feel the possessing demon and may even deny that one exists.[4]

Such demonic possessions, Skinner explains, can be compared to other, more common instances in which the person having such an experience is either unaware of it, or unable to feel it. In the same way in which a possessed person does not feel the possessing demon, an intelligent person does not feel their intelligence, an introverted person does not feel their introversion, a speaker does not feel the grammatical rules that apply to their speech, and as Skinner refers to Freud, these concepts that we do not feel are byproducts and not causes for our behavior.[5]

Skinner attempts to eradicate these ideas of an internal, abstract humanism by the call for the abolition of man, referring to C. S Lewis' concept. To Skinner, it is high time to stop thinking about this needed procedure as an attempt at eliminating "Man in his humanity," but rather that "What is being abolished is autonomous man — the inner man, the homunculus, the possessing demon, the man defended by the literatures of freedom and dignity."[6]

Skinner attempts not only to upset the balance between internal agency and external influence, but rather to have the latter completely take over the former. This claim, then, leaves mankind to the merciless, uncaring and inhuman hands of the world, endlessly dissolving and conjoining the human race. This decision takes place, even if symbolically, in *The Matrix*, when Cipher betrays his friends and chooses to forget everything he knows and be put back in the matrix. In this scene we see Cipher, in his last "Internal" and conscious decision, as he chooses to eliminate his freedom and dignity, to quote Skinner, and become wholly immersed and affected by the externality of the matrix. On first glance, this pact between Cipher and Agent Smith does seem like a pact with the devil. Cipher wants to go back to the matrix as a rich person in the same way that other magicians demanded vast riches from the devil. Cipher pays, we can then say, not (only) by betraying his friends (committing a sin), but by surrendering his eternal afterlife, or his digital existence, to Satan. However, this pact is not made in order to corrupt Cipher and take him away from God, but in order to maintain the immanent, uncaring, demonic presence that controls humanity.

When Cipher is re-possessed by the matrix, he will not be able to feel this possession.

Notes

1. Skinner, B. F., *Beyond Freedom and Dignity*. Harmondsworth: Penguin Books, 1976, p. 196.
2. Marlowe, Christopher, *Doctor Faustus*, John D. Jump (ed.). London: Routledge, 2005, pp. 111–112.
3. Skinner, B. F., *Beyond Freedom and Dignity*. Harmondsworth: Penguin Books, 1976, p. 19.
4. Ibid., p. 21.
5. Ibid.
6. Ibid., p. 196.

3.

Mighty Darkness

> Panthea: I see a mighty darkness, Filling the seat of power, and rays of gloom Dart round, as light from the meridian sun, Ungazed upon and shapeless; neither limb, nor form, nor outline; yet we feel it is A living Spirit.
>
> Percy Bysshe Shelley, *Prometheus Unbound*.[1]

While the world is certainly not human, it is also certainly not entirely demonic. Instead, it is populated, and can be populated even more, with entities, attractors and phenomena that can be thought of as demonic. The Jewish Talmud tells us that if we could see the numerous demons that populate the universe, our existence could not be possible.[2] In this sense, the full knowledge of the potential hostility of an uncaring universe can, and has indeed been described, even felt, by writers and philosophers alike. In the seventeenth century, the mere idea of an endless, godless universe had Blaise Pascal stricken with horror, describing the silence of these infinite spaces as terrifying.[3] Professor Avihu Zakai describes how the disenchantment of the world, with the dawn of the new physics of the heavens that was wrought unto the cosmos by Copernicus, Kepler and Galileo, left Pascal alienated and filled with dread, as such a universe leaves him without any knowledge as of the purpose of his existence.[4] Such reaction, Zakai writes, signifies the sense of loss in the elimination of both the universe of Dante and the glorious, geocentric and anthropocentric universe that was formed around the purpose of mankind's redemption.[5]

However, as Zakai points out, it was not merely the endlessness of space that horrified Pascal. It was also the attempts at a new rational philosophy of nature, meaning a new way to understand the universe without God.[6] Pascal, then, is standing helplessly between the infinite, godless chasm that the universe is revealed to be, and its new illumination by godless thinkers.

But there is a big difference between an infinite, godless universe and a universe populated with demons. In the nineteenth century, H. P. Lovecraft's literature made the idea of cosmic horror popular, to this day, by telling of a universe that does not see humanity or worse, does not care about humanity. Unlike Pascal's universe, Lovecraft had in mind a universe that justifies the human fear of it, claiming, as Eugene Thacker quotes and then elaborates, that the oldest human emotion is fear, and the oldest fear is the fear from the unknown. This is where, as Thacker then writes, that:

> Horror is about the paradoxical thought of the unthinkable. In so far as it deals with this limit of thought, encapsulated in the phrase of the world-without-us, horror is "philosophical." But in so far as it evokes the world-without-us as a limit, it is a "negative philosophy" (akin to negative theology, but in the absence of God).[7]

While Pascal may fear the possible eradication of theology through the sheer vastness of the universe, as well as by science's much more successful method of illuminating and understanding it, Thacker suggests a negative philosophy to accompany negative theology, by which the universe remains ever-dark; ever-horrific. If, in Cary Wolfe's introduction to the book *The Parasite* by Michel Serres, we read that post-humanism takes place when the human is "finally eclipsed by various technological, informatic, and bioengineering developments,"[8] then Thacker offers a sense of doom to a similar notion of *Cosmic* Pessimism,[9] the idea that "We do not live, we are lived."[10]

We are lived by exterior forces that affect our behavior. We are lived by Descartes' demon. We are lived, sometimes, through messages that harm, or even destroy their medium; Us.

In order to move past the mere theoretical assumption, thus making this form of demonology relevant to today, rather than a mere historical curiosity, another concept discussed by Thacker, and that which could be then compared to Pascal's concept of the godless universe, should be brought to light — that of divine darkness. Thacker suggests two mystical limits within this form of darkness. The first is "the limit of human knowing," meaning a limit between that which is human and that which is not human, but "may still be invested with being, order, and meaning." This limit, then, suggests a "derivative knowing of this unknowing." The second barrier, described by Thacker as "The limit of the limit," is the absolute barrier of the human ability to know, suggesting a double negativity — that there is nothing beyond this limit, and that this nothing cannot be known.[11] Thacker applies this form of darkness to mystical texts, but such darkness is present in the physical world as well, both around the human and within the human. To begin with the godless universe that horrified Pascal, we can think about the non-human universe around us, the non-human limit between mankind and the immense chasm of non-humanity, ever expanding and never, we can assume, completely understood by humans. This universe, however, is the *observable* universe, beyond which lies the *unobservable* universe, expanding and moving away from us faster than the speed of light, thus forever beyond human knowledge. Is there anything beyond that immense chasm of the *unobservable* universe? All we can guess is that there is nothing, and that this nothing is unknowable.

But while this astronomical description of the universe does indeed justify Pascal's dread by making the already dark universe even darker, it does not exemplify a demonic presence in the sense that is discussed here, meaning as an immanent, anti-human negation. It does not, unless such nothingness can emerge within our observable reality. On my bookshelf, there is an old book published by National Geographic, titled *Man's Conquest of Space*. Regardless how fascinating the exploration of space is to me and of how impressive it must be to take part in such exploration, the term conquest sounds hasty, if not completely naïve, as even the full humanization of the Milky Way galaxy, an aim that we can say is not close to even being conceivable, will be almost meaningless in terms of thinking about deep space in its entirety. There might be, however, a different presence that might be conquering space as we speak, doing it much more efficiently. This presence is a presence of negation that can be well thought of as demonic.

Being careful not to fall into the trap of "Quantum Woo," meaning not to abuse the lack of understanding in quantum mechanics in order to try and prove supernatural phenomena, one such theory can indeed give an example for an immanent, negating darkness — the transition from *False Vacuum* to *True Vacuum*. In this unlikely, yet possible scenario, the very physics of the universe might produce a bubble of true vacuum that will expand at a speed close to the speed of light, annihilating everything in its wake.[12] However unlikely, such an event may have already taken place somewhere distant in the universe, or it might erupt somewhere nearby without any warning. An annihilating entity, such as an ever-growing bubble of true vacuum, not only signifies a nothingness that cannot be known, but it also makes this nothingness take over everything that could be known. This possibility of an ouroboros-like universe, that might suddenly turn on itself and devour everything within it, can certainly confront mankind with an unknowable nothingness. Yet while it might be considered demonic in the sense that this theoretical phenomenon exists as a form of negation for our world, it still does not reside within the human mind. In other words, this phenomenon does not possess humans, even if it has the potential of completely wiping out any living creature. Indeed, space holds many unthinkable dangers to mankind, bringing to mind the moment from the movie *Interstellar* (Nolan, 2014), in which after losing two decades in a time dilation due to extreme proximity to a black hole, pilot, Joseph Cooper, says to astronomer, Dr Amelia Brand, that we, mankind, are not prepared for space travel.

We are not prepared, because venturing into the vast chasm of nothingness might become the doom of all mankind, not because of a lethal phenomenon of negation, but because the new conditions might alter the thoughts and behavior of mankind into negating itself into extinction. This danger is described by author and professor of political science, Daniel Deudney, in his book *Dark Skies*.[13] In this book, Deudney warns against space exploration, claiming that it is space expansionism, the shift from a planetary-scale to an interplanetary-scale mankind, that could bring the end of the human race by the hands of the human race. In essence, then, we can say that it is the very venture into the non-human, the black chasm, that will ultimately turn mankind into devouring itself. As Deudney remarks, the moon landing was lamented by C. S. Lewis "for allowing Fallen Man to spread damage across the universe,"[14] but the danger described here flows in the opposite direction — not from fallen man to other words, but from the new reality of space expansionism, into the behavior and fate of mankind.

Deudney lists several dangers that can be put in three categories. The first category is of dangers that already exist in our time, and which are going to be amplified as space expansionism progresses. The second category is of dangers that are currently being withheld and contained but are likely to erupt once mankind spreads throughout the solar system. The last category is that of wholly new dangers that do not exist today but are likely to emerge in the future. The dangers that Deudney lists, regarding serious threats to the fundamentals of humanity, do not include those of malfunctions, such as the dangers of low gravity and how living in space could affect childbirth, for instance. While Deudney mentions these probable problems,[15] he notes that these are not the critical dangers he is worried about. As he writes, "The greatest calamities will come from success, not failure."[16]

Dangers that already threaten mankind here on earth, and that can be amplified through space expansionism are the rise of dictatorships[17] and the use of nuclear or biological warfare, for instance.[18] Not only that these powerful weapons could be created and used without any regulation, but an even more destructive weapon could be employed in space, the use of whole asteroids as weapons.[19] Other dangers are being restrained here on earth, but will probably be produced in space, such as lethal nano technology, or an artificial super intelligence.[20] In the third category, Deudney points at two dangers that are currently unknown and non-existent to mankind, but might emerge in space. The first danger is listed as "Monster Multiplication," meaning that with the "increased scope of geographic and technology interactions with adverse unknowable effects" comes the "increased probability of unknowingly triggering large-scale disasters"[21] (note that Deudney does not discuss the possibility of discovering alien life in this book). The other danger is termed "species radiation," meaning that with its expansion into space, and to numerous different celestial bodies such as the moon, Mars, Saturn's moons and numerous asteroids, these alien environments and their effects on the human population, together with gene manipulation done in order to adapt to these places, and with the possible "cyborgization" of humans, mankind as a unified biological race might cease to exist, disintegrating into numerous species that are no longer human.[22]

Deudney does not see a way to completely prevent space exploration, even with these existential threats lurking beyond Earth's atmosphere. To him, "Perhaps the only saving grace of this key conclusion of geopolitical analysis is that the demons loosened by opening the Pandora's box of space colonization might start to wreak their damage early enough to throttle the colonial enterprise before it gets too fatally under way."[23] Essentially, we can consider as demonic presence the pulling of mankind into space exploration and the then-inevitable emergence of alien monstrosities that will replace those who were once humans. In the darkness of dead space, not only will there be no God, there also won't be any humans either. Here, space expansionism and astrophysics merge with demonology, showing how black space takes mankind into its vast emptiness, changing the entire human species and driving it into extinction. In space, a new word emerges, as Deudney suggests the term *Astrocide* as the idea of the extinction of mankind, directly or indirectly due to human space expansionism,[24] an eventual process that mankind cannot resist but go through. The universe, uncaring, proves to be demonic, and those who dare venture into it will not come back the same. To Deudney's theoretical and scientific analysis, one can find echoes of Lovecraft's famous warning:

> The most merciful thing in the world, I think, is the inability of the human mind to correlate all its contents. We live on a placid island of ignorance in the midst of black seas of infinity, and it was not meant that we should voyage far. The sciences, each straining in its own direction, have hitherto harmed us little; but some day the piecing together of dissociated knowledge will open up such terrifying vistas of reality, and of our frightful position therein, that we shall either go mad from the revelation or flee from the deadly light into the peace and safety of a new dark age.[25]

Pascal was horrified by the idea of an endless, godless space. Later theories brought to mind the possibility of nothingness erupting in space and annihilating everything in its wake. In Deudney's projection, space does not need to be endless in order to carry the seeds of self-destruction into the mind of man, and there is one more example of a demon haunting the mind, in which outer space need not be at all. On a long enough timeline, as they say, anyone browsing on social media of any sort will come across claims according to which the Earth is flat, there is no real gravity and "space" is an enclosed bubble in which planets revolve around a stationed flat world. The details of this cosmogony, varied from one flat-earth account to another, are not as important as the idea itself and the way it spreads around.

The cosmogony of the flat earth is essentially a religious one, as it involves an intelligent design of an unnatural formation of the cosmos. Not only is it religious, it is fundamentally Gnostic, as it involves the powers of darkness that hide this truth from us, obscuring not only the true design of the cosmos, but also its creator. There are many religious, spiritual and mythological designs and ideas of cosmogony, and in theory the idea of the flat earth should not have been any different. It is different, however, because it is based not on belief, but on attempts to draw empirical conclusions from observation and from scientific inquiry. This puts the idea of flat earth in a peculiar position, as it is trying to replace conservative and careful scientific observation with paranoid pseudoscience that is based solely on ignorance and the disintegration of true scientific observation, deduction and inductive reasoning. One might ask how come such paranoid theories manage to go viral. Ideas about the flat earth propagate by either of two ways. The first is the claim that every heliocentric observation is at least flawed, if not a downright viciously produced lie. This includes every one of NASA's images of the universe, or every video taken from a satellite or a space station, from which the earth seems like a sphere. Together with this evidence, gravity is eliminated as well, as it cannot take place in a conservative physical way on a flat surface. The second method is by offering an alternative cosmogony, in which the size of off-world bodies, their orbit, distance and compositions are changed. We are left, then, with a cosmogony that not only cannot fully explain itself but also negates the well-explained mainstream cosmogony. To answer the question of how such a paranoid idea can then grow so much in popularity, I would suggest that the answer lies exactly in its integral paranoia. Essentially, we can think about the idea of the flat earth not merely as an idea, but as a phenomenon that spreads through texts and images, replacing reason with fear and a logical analysis with paranoid fundamentalism. While the idea of global moral progress is certainly questionable, the idea of a global accumulation of knowledge and that of the progress of technology is a sound one. But inside the intricate system of ideas, creativity, thought and behavior through which we exist, the idea of the flat earth does not merely offer a demonstrative call of protest, such as the likes of traditionalism or even Luddism, but rather a viral, negating counter movement of the disintegration of factual knowledge and of reason. This could be, then, the demonic manipulation by Descartes' demon. Reasoning dethroned, paranoia reigns supreme.

Notes

1. Shelley, Percy Bysshe, *Prometheus Unbound, A Lyrical Drama*. Boston: D. C. Heath & Co., 1892, p. 63.
2. Talmud, Brachot 6:1.
3. Pascal, Blaise, *Pensées and Other Writings*, Honor Levi (trans.). Oxford: Oxford University Press, 1999, p. 73.
4. Zakai, Avihu, *The Disenchantment of the World: Science and Religion in the Early Modern Period*. Tel Aviv: Resling, 2018, pp. 153–154.

5. Ibid., p. 154.
6. Ibid.
7. Thacker, Eugene, *In the Dust of this Planet: Horror of Philosophy,* Vol. 1, Winchester: Zero Books, 2011, p. 14.
8. Serres, Michel, *The Parasite,* Lawrence R. Schehr (trans.). Minneapolis: University of Minneapolis Press, 2007, p. xi.
9. Thacker, Eugene, *Cosmic Pessimism*. Minneapolis: Univocal Publishing, 2015.
10. Ibid., p. 23.
11. Thacker, Eugene, *Starry Speculative Corpse: Horror of Philosophy* Vol.2. Winchester: Zero Books, 2015, pp. 41–42.
12. Tegmark, Max, and Nick Bostrom, "Is a Doomsday Catastrophe Likely?" *Nature* (London) 438, no. 7069 (2005): p. 754. https://doi.org/10.1038/438754a.
13. Deudney, Daniel, *Dark Skies: Space Expansionism, Planetary Geopolitics & the End of Humanity*. New York: Oxford University Press, 2020.
14. Ibid., p. 6.
15. Ibid., p. 335.
16. Ibid.
17. Ibid., pp. 347–350.
18. Ibid., p. 338.
19. Ibid., pp. 339–340.
20. Ibid., p. 358.
21. Ibid.
22. Ibid., pp. 340–342.
23. Ibid., p. 358.
24. Ibid., p. 362.
25. Lovecraft, H. P., *The Call of Cthulhu and Other Weird Stories,* S. T. Joshi (ed.). London: Penguin Books, 2002, p. 139.

4.
Rat-Man

> A final question is urgently posed: "how to get the humans in these systems to participate in the plan?" His answers do not lie in persuasion or education but in behavioral modification. He says we need "new predictive theories of human decision making" as well as "incentive mechanism design," an idea that is comparable to Skinner's "schedules of reinforcement." Regarding how to get humans to follow the plan, Pentland offers the principle of "social influence" to explain the design mechanisms through which millions of human beings can be herded toward the guaranteed outcomes of safety, stability, and efficiency. He refers to his own studies, in which "the problems of industry and government" can largely be explained by the pattern of information transfer, especially how people influence and mimic one another.
>
> Shoshana Zuboff, *The Age of Surveillance Capitalism*.[1]

As an animal liberation activist, and during the years I worked as the coordinator of activity of the *Israeli Society for the Abolition of Vivisection*, I came across different articles about two specific experiments on rats, which to me were more shocking and horrific than other experiments inflicted by humans on rats, or any other non-human animal. When we read about these experiments, it is easy, even tempting, to read them as experiments that reveal hidden areas in the wiring of the rat's brain. This is because we, even those who oppose the experiments, automatically side with the actions of the human researchers merely by understanding, more or less and without delving into technical details, what they actually performed. But while the humanistic mechanics of the experiments are indeed evident, we can now read these experiments as truly demonic. These experiments take place for their own perspective of necessity, regardless of their victim's will, by penetrating the victim's mind, and by doing so destroying it.

The first experiment can in fact be separated into two, both revolving around the ability to remotely control rats' minds and actions. Of these two experiments, the first involved connecting the brain of a rat to a remote control, enabling a person with a laptop to control the rat's movement through a maze from afar.[2] Is this a case of Descartes' demon produced in a lab? On this experiment, Slavoj Zizék writes:

> For the first time, the 'will' of a living animal agent, its 'spontaneous' decisions about the movements it makes, were taken over by an external machine. Of course, the great philosophical question here is how the unfortunate rat 'experienced' these movements decided from outside: did it continue to 'experience' them as spontaneous (in other words, was it totally unaware that its movements were being steered?), or was it aware that something was wrong? And, maybe, therein resides the difference between Chinese citizens and us, free citizens of the Western liberal countries: the Chinese human rats are at least aware they are controlled, while we are the stupid rats strolling around unaware of how our movements are monitored.[3]

World politics aside, Zizék points to the possibility of externally controlling the minds of others, with and without their ability to know that they are being manipulated. There is, however, a difference between the unaware citizen and the unaware rat. While the unaware citizen is a victim of suggestions and manipulations by means of language perceived by the senses, the rat has an alien presence inside the brain, erupting from inside the mind and out to the rest of its body. Here, the second experiment of this sort makes things more horrific and more demonic, as the message that penetrates the mind of the rat does indeed bring its negation, not only as an autonomous being but also as a rat. In this experiment, rats that had electrodes attached to their brains were remotely programmed to attack and kill other living beings.[4]

The second type of experiment was not about turning the rat into a remote-controlled object, but about turning the rat onto itself. In this experiment, rats learned that by pressing a lever in their cage, they can feel instant pleasure. This pleasure was inflicted upon them by researchers by connecting a device to the rats' reward system in their brains, causing the rats to:

> [...] work continuously — lever-pressing at rates of several thousand responses per hour — for days to obtain direct electrical stimulation of the lateral hypothalamus and related brain regions. They do so to the exclusion of other behaviors, starving themselves for the opportunity to self-stimulate if food and stimulation are concurrently available for only a limited portion of each day. Once experienced with the stimulation, rats will cross electrified grids to gain access to the lever, accepting higher shock to obtain stimulation than they are willing to accept to obtain food (even when deprived for 24 hr).[5]

In this experiment, we can say that the rat is being short-circuited not only into forgetting about its "ratness," but also into forgetting that it is a living being, neglecting the very basic fundaments of any living being on earth — the need for food. The rat, by technological means, becomes an ouroboros, biting its own self to death. Unlike the slaughterhouse, in which the human blindness towards animal suffering and will to live is complete, the research lab offers a paradoxical examination of the non-human subject. On the one hand, the animal is examined carefully for its reactions, pain and behavior during the procedure. On the other hand, the animal's distress is not a moral issue as much as it is a procedural issue that may or may not have consequences on the experiment itself. Thus, the comparison of such an experiment to a demonic activity within the rat's brain is not merely metaphorical. True, we don't know what it's like to be a rat. But to the rat, the short circuiting of its brain is beyond its ability to understand, as it becomes a victim to an external force that, while attacking the rat and feeding off its effect on its victim, is uncaring for the rat's well-being.

Lurking for millennia, buried deep inside the potential of mankind to manipulate living beings, the event in which several human beings short-circuit a rat by connecting it to its own brain and detaching it from anything else, emerges in the twentieth century, as the moral, technological and mental conditions make it surface, as if it was an artefact buried under ice for centuries before being revealed by the rising temperatures. This event, taking place inside a laboratory, is then multiplied and copies itself into more such events. It is made known by images and texts, driving other researchers — who may have never thought of doing so before reading about the experiment — to perform similar demonic rituals. As this one event becomes a legion of similar performances, countless more animals are being possessed by such procedures, losing their minds and driven down to their death.

The fusing of the human and the non-human together, by body, mind or will, has been the subject of many wonders and monstrosities throughout history. Long before the animal-human gods of ancient Egypt, statues such as the Lion-man of Hohlenstein-Stadel, a statue of a lion-man that was found in 1939 and believed to be about 40,000 years old, were made. Not only gods, but also monsters — beings such as werewolves were (and are) not uncommon in folklore and literature. In the same book in which King James discusses the true existence of demons, he also denies the existence of werewolves, offering a more rational reason for the belief in them, rather than claiming that men can indeed transform into animals.[6] But the fusion of humans and non-humans, or the attempts of such hybrids, will probably never vanish. In his book *Black Mass*, John Gray writes about the Soviet attempt to create a super soldier, performed by a horse breeder named Ilya Ivanov under the command of Stalin, who "wanted a new breed of soldier — 'a new invincible human being', highly resistant to pain, that needed little food or sleep."[7] A more peaceful, voluntary idea of such welding together of different species, albeit to the eventual complete disintegration of mankind into countless other hybrid-species, is discussed in Donna Harraway's *Staying with the Trouble*,[8] and in Patricia MacCormack's *The Ahuman Manifesto*.[9]

Among the countless superheroes and supervillains who embody, in comic books and on the screen, the fusing together of the human and the non-human, one movie offers a complete opposite for the demonic experiment in which rats are being short-circuited. In the animated film *Ratatouille* (Bird, 2007), it is a rat, proficient in the art of cooking, who controls, albeit not by any violent means, the mind of a human, an untalented kitchen worker, thus helping him to create wonderful dishes at the restaurant. An animated fiction aimed at children, this story is a story about a symbiosis between two beings, about the possible achievement of knowledge and abilities by being connected to an exterior agent. A wholly different fantasy about a human-rat connection is found in Freud's case of the "Rat Man."[10] In this case, Freud's patient, Ernst Lanzer, was haunted by a story he once heard, about a torturing method from the East. As Freud documents the session with his patient, who reluctantly told him of the story, not even being able to utter the words in order to fully describe it:

> I went on to say that I would do all I could, nevertheless, to guess the full meaning of any hints he gave me. Was he perhaps thinking of impalement? 'No, not that; ... the criminal was tied up ...' — he expressed himself so indistinctly that I could not immediately guess in what position ... a pot was turned upside down on his buttocks ... some rats were put into it ... and they ... 'he had again got up, and was showing every sign of horror and resistance' ... bored their way in .. . 'Into his anus, I helped him out'.[11]

The morbid vision of this torturing method haunts Freud's patient, together with other extreme thoughts and behaviors, such as the impulse to cut his own throat with a blade. And while for Freud the rats signify inner meanings regarding the patient's life, the idea of numerous rats, a legion of beings penetrating the body and gnawing through it can also reflect the demonic multiplicity of alien beings, violently yet helplessly taking over the human body.

Notes

1. Zuboff, Shoshana, *The Age of Surveillance Capitalism: The Fight for a Human Future at the New Frontier of Power*. New York: Public Affairs, 2019, pp. 401–402.
2. For example, read: Harder, Ben, "Scientists 'Drive' Rats By Remote Control," in *National Geographic* May 1, 2002. Retrieved from: https://web.archive.org/web/20020609184541/http://news.nationalgeographic.com/news/2002/05/0501_020501_roborats.html.

3. Zizék, Slavoj, *Trouble in Paradise: From the End of History to the End of Capitalism*. UK: Penguin Books, 2015, p. 60.
4. As shown here: https://www.youtube.com/watch?v=Zdgw4S0GgL8.
5. Wise R. A., "Brain reward circuitry: insights from unsensed incentives," *Neuron*. 36 (2): 229–40, p. 231 (October 2022). doi:10.1016/s0896-6273(02)00965-0.
6. Tyson, Donald, *The Demonology of King James I*. Woodbury: Llewellyn Publications, 2011, p. 153.
7. Gray John, *Black Mass: How Religion Led the World into Crisis*. London: Penguin Books, 2008, p. 58.
8. Harraway, Donna J., *Staying with the Trouble: Making Kin in the Chthulucene*. Durham: Duke University Press, 2016.
9. MacCormack, Patricia, *The Ahuman Manifesto: Activism for the End of the Anthropocene*. London: Bloomsbury Academic, 2020.
10. Strachey, James (ed.), *The Standard Edition of the Complete Psychological Works of Sigmund Freud*, James Stachey (trans.). London: The Hogarth Press, 1981.
11. Ibid., p. 166.

The Message That Duplicates Itself

1.

Trigger Warning

> "Then you don't believe in numerologies of any kind," Diotallevi said, disappointed.
>
> "On the contrary, I believe firmly. I believe the universe is a great symphony of numerical correspondences, I believe that numbers and their symbolisms provide a path to special knowledge. But if the world, below and above, is a system of correspondences where tout se tient [everything fits together], it's natural for the kiosk and the pyramid, both works of man, to reproduce in their structure, unconsciously, the harmonies of the cosmos. The so-called pyramidologists discover with their incredibly tortuous methods a straightforward truth, a truth far more ancient, and one already known. It is the logic of research and discovery that is tortuous, because it is the logic of science. Whereas the logic of knowledge needs no discovery, because it knows already. Why must it demonstrate that which could not be otherwise? If there is a secret, it is much more profound. These authors of yours remain simply on the surface. I imagine this one also repeats all the tales of how the Egyptians knew about electricity..."
>
> Umberto Eco, *Foucault's Pendulum*.[1]

On the first day of 1984, *The New York Times* published an article by Edmond Van den Bossche, regarding George Orwell's 1949 book, *1984*. Was Orwell's famous book just another false prophecy? To think that would be silly. As Van den Bossche writes:

> "1984" is a political statement. It contains no prophetic declaration, only a simple warning to mankind. Orwell did not believe that 35 years after the publication of his book, the world would be ruled by Big Brother, but he often proclaimed that 1984 could happen if man did not become aware of the assaults on his personal freedom and did not defend his most precious right, the right to have his own thoughts.[2]

For Orwell, there was indeed a need for warning, as he discloses in a letter written in 1944, just a few years before the publication of *1984*. Orwell opens this letter by writing:

> I must say I believe, or fear, that taking the world as a whole these things are on the increase. Hitler, no doubt, will soon disappear, but only at the expense of strengthening (a) Stalin, (b) the Anglo-American millionaires and (c) all sorts of petty fuhrers of the type of de Gaulle. All the national movements everywhere, even those that originate in resistance to German domination, seem to take non-democratic forms, to group themselves round some superhuman fuhrer (Hitler, Stalin, Salazar, Franco, Gandhi, De Valera are all varying examples) and to adopt the theory that the end justifies the means. Everywhere the world movement seems to be in the direction of centralised economies which can be made to 'work' in an economic sense but which are not democratically organised and which tend to establish a caste system. With this go the horrors of emotional nationalism and a tendency to disbelieve in the existence of objective truth because all

> the facts have to fit in with the words and prophecies of some infallible fuhrer.[3]

It wouldn't be hard to imagine the anticipation that had probably grown since the publication of Orwell's book, to the coming of the year 1984, as warnings about the future can be met with either criticism and scorn, or with fear and belief, not merely for their contents but for the time stamp attached to them. Decades after 1984, Orwell's book is still regarded not only as a tremendously important work of literature, but also as a warning for a world that came true, came true only partially or might come true soon enough.

On the other hand, it is difficult to consider the dystopian world of the Netflix series *Black Mirror* as a proper warning from a dystopian future (or present), as it replaces critical warning with entertainment. Rather than a portrayal of a horrifying future, *Black Mirror* thrives on a sense of dark temptation, a spectacle that transforms danger into pleasure and the specific technical details of human inferiority to the totalitarianism of technology into creative ideas for the next successful episode. Essentially, then, while *1984* warns directly against dictatorship and the controlling of the mind through language, *Black Mirror* turns mankind's dissolution into the technological to a form of entertainment.

1984 is clearly a dystopian novel and here lies an important difference with *Black Mirror*. The ideas of Utopia and Dystopia share the common ground that is the complete and permanent human control over nature. These ideas are attached to each other even further, as no true utopia is possible since there will always be someone who will consider it dystopian. Hence, we are left with what seems like a polarity between total benevolence and total malevolence, both achieved by complete anthropocentric control over the world, turning the idea of resistance or revolution into a romantic fantasy at best.

The historical struggles concerning the distribution of power through mankind need not be reminded here, but their concept is nevertheless clear — these are struggles about the direction of power, about the duality of good and evil. Good can be God, good can be a certain political system. Bad can be the devil, bad can be a certain political system.

This dogmatic and redundant polarity, that which satanism offers, is described in the book *Revolutionary Demonology*, written by the collective Gruppo di Nun:

> Contemporary satanism in its entirety is nothing but a reinterpretation of the dogmatic principles of the Right Hand Path, clothed in new garments so as to attract the interest of new groups of potential initiates. It is therefore not surprising to note that many forms of satanism are often accompanied by an obsession with power, an exaltation of the individual, and a frantic negation of the existence of God which becomes an affirmation of one's own individual divinity. This satanism is in no way structurally different from the religion it wants to oppose; it proposes, in an ultra-simplified and, in all probability, scarcely effective way, the same dogmas and practices to which the Western Hermetic tradition has always referred.[4]

Through this brief description, we can read *1984* as a story about a satanist distribution of power, not for God, not for the people, but rather for a specific party and a specific party leader, regardless of the question of whether this leader is fictional or real. In Orwell's story we read about the protagonist who, even if for a brief period of time, seems to undermine the totality of the party's control over what it means to be human. Throughout most of this dark story, we, the readers, are assured that there is someone who can fight and prevail even against the worst kind of totalitarianism. Winston Smith, the protagonist of *1984*, fails. But for a brief period of time, he is a superhero that, while lacking any exceptional power, does not fall short of heroes such as Constantine, Neo and Wick, each fighting against a different system of oppression. In the tragic novel, Satan prevails. Yet like the other three protagonists, Winston Smith is taking a path not only for the liberation of mankind, but for his own deification as a hero — a doctrine that, as described by Gruppo di Nun, is fundamental to every Western hermetic tradition of the right-hand path.[5]

In the world of *Black Mirror*, on the other hand, there are no longer protagonist magicians who can act in the world. Instead, with each episode in the series, mankind seems to fall further into the darkness of an uncaring technological reign of algorithms and digital platforms, losing its sovereignty over the body, over the mind and over the uniqueness of both. The adversary in the TV series, then, is not satanic in the sense of an individual enemy who shifts all power to its hands. Instead, these are demons, disintegrating the will of humans and turning them into themselves by penetrating their self-sovereignty. Through its technological orientation, the TV series portrays humans who succumb to a form of darkness, to the disillusion of man's power over himself or the world. In a way there emerges a sense of an anti-utopia, meaning mankind's inevitable loss to the dominance of nature, only in *Black Mirror* there is no longer nature, but forms of technology that become quasi-supernatural.

Thus, unlike *1984*, the TV series *Black Mirror* can be read as demonological in the sense that is hinted by Gruppo di Nun in the following passages:

> How can we reach a darkness so radically and frighteningly alien to everything we know? How can we think of approaching its black fire without being destroyed? She is singularity; we understand the

> necessity of Her existence, but we can never guess at the enormity of Her wonder. We know Her from the stories of men as an immense anthropophagous serpent which, every night, threatens to forever swallow the Sun and its light, plunging the world into an eternal twilight; and in these same stories, every night the serpent is defeated, so that the Sun can return to shine once again.
>
> But no sun burns forever. Any god who promises salvation is lying, because there is no salvation in the jaws of the Beast. Whoever receives the bite of the serpent knows true terror, and, in the darkness of her womb, meets Love and is reborn to a new life. Cosmic Love is by definition a suicidal love; only while we fall inexorably into our dissolution can we fulfil our destiny and shine.[6]

One difference is striking, however. While Gruppo di Nun's darkness is mystical, theological and astrophysical, the majority of *Black Mirror*'s episodes involve strictly the effect of technology on mankind. The anti-humanist agent in the series, the demonology of *Black Mirror*, involves a mixture between deterministic entropy and a Lovecraftian monstrosity, albeit man-made and earthly. Nevertheless, it does retain a sense of supernatural wonder or horror, bringing to mind several stories from an older TV show, an older incarnation of this program, *The Twilight Zone*. Indeed, the horror in *Black Mirror* emerges not from that which is *above* nature (magic, aliens etc.), and not from that which is natural (natural disasters, epidemics, an evil antagonist), but from that which was created by mankind, only to become too powerful and too menacing. The horror in *Black Mirror* is not a supernatural horror, but a *subnatural* horror. Mankind is threatened from above, by the supernatural, non-human, cosmic, diabolic and so forth, and from below, by the subnatural, by agents which are man-made yet uncontrollable, unfathomable, uncaring, hostile and horrific.

There is no escape from the subnatural, demonic entropy. *Black Mirror* demonstrates the futility of resistance by engulfing both the message and the medium, through an arc that can be drawn between several episodes, not as a warning, but as a message that seems to devour its medium, the viewer. The episode "Fifteen Million Merits" (Season 01, Episode 02, Lyn, 2011) takes place in a world of strict hierarchy that is detached from our own world. In this episode, the human world is divided among several social classes. At the lowest there are the cleaners, all are overweight and unfit to fill the role of the medium class. They wear yellow and are often mocked and abused by the middle class. In the middle class there are the majority of the population, the cyclists. These people are wearing gray and spend their days cycling on stationary bicycles, generating the electricity needed for the world. At the highest class there are the celebrities and influencers, who enjoy the most freedom. In this episode we see the protagonist, Bing. After realizing that the girl he loved and encouraged to compete in order to become a famous singer, was maliciously manipulated and convinced to become a porn star, he has a plan against the hierarchical society. Much like Winston Smith, albeit in a more colorful and entertainment-oriented world, he is working his way to reach the most sensitive place in his world — the talent competition that serves as the one and only meaning to life — a threshold that separates future celebrities from the rest of the population. There, his masterplan is finally revealed. While we are led to believe that Bing plans a violent attack against the judges, he merely wants to voice an authentic opinion about the society in which he lives — a society that has lost all means of authenticity. Then, Bing fails and is swallowed by the great beast. His authenticity rewards him with a streaming program of his own, making him an influencer by removing any further traces of authenticity and absorbing whatever resistance he might have posed to the system. In effect, Bing learns to love the big brother, but in this story, it is a non-existent, demonic brother.

Robert Segal wrote that, regarding the violent story of Oedipus killing his father and marrying his mother, two people enjoy such disaster. These two victimizers are the person who is telling the story and the person who is listening to it.[7] In this sense, *Black Mirror* thrives on our attraction to the grim future (or present) it reflects. In the interactive episode "Bandersnatch" (Slade, 2018), an episode that deals with the ideas of free will, we think that the protagonist is a young programmer, Stefan Butler. However, when Butler appears to contact us viewers and have a short conversation with the people who watch the episode, we can understand that those responsible for his self-destruction are us. Butler thinks that he can do whatever he wants, but with each decision to be made in this interactive episode, there are very limited choices offered by the makers of this episode for us viewers to choose from. What does this mean about us? Are we really free to choose from an unlimited pool of possibilities? Baudrillard writes that even a person who decides to live his life through the randomness of a dice roll, condemned to obey whatever the random roll of it will say, still has to first decide what each face of the dice means.[8] In this way, we are merely given few options by the writers of Bandersnatch when we control (or when we *think* we control?) Stefan Butler. When Butler realizes that he is nothing but a simulated character, condemned to obey us viewers, he eventually embraces his fate like we embrace the set of options that we are given while playing in this interactive episode. When he asks us who we are, one of the options allows us to identify ourselves as the streaming network Netflix. While this does not say much to Butler, who lives in the 1980s, this answer does bind us with the platform that broadcasts this episode for us. *Black Mirror* is no longer shown *to* us. It *is* us. At this point, then, an even grimmer and more realistic version of the story told in "Fifteen Million Merits" can be shown through the episode "Smithereens" (Season 05, Episode 02, Hawes, 2019). In this episode, protagonist Chris Gillhaney goes on a more violent journey in order to be able to make his voice heard by the CEO of the social media platform "Smithereens." His tragic story regarding the addictive programming of social networks is heard in an emotional moment, after which he is shot dead, and nothing is changed. We are now sided with digital platforms rather than with the will for authenticity.

But the message of authentic resistance truly dies in the episode "Joan is Awful" (Season 06, Episode 01, Pankiw, 2023). In this episode, Joan realizes that her life is being recorded and broadcast in the worst possible way to portray her, by a streaming service called "Streamberry," which is indeed very reminiscent of the streaming service Netflix. Putting the rest of the story aside, one might consider this episode a blatant, rude and real protest against the streaming corporation, but if on "Bandersnatch" *Black Mirror* merged with the viewers, it now merges with the streaming service. In other words, when Netflix shows such harsh criticism against itself, it means that this criticism no longer exists as criticism, but as entertainment. So, regarding the context of this book, one can say that *Black Mirror* is certainly not a message that harmed its medium, the streaming service. But with the coagulation of *Black Mirror* with Netflix, the entire complex becomes the message, and we become the medium, changed in that resistance and protest no longer seem to us as authentic ways to oppose power, but merely as forms of yet more layered entertainment.

Everything decays to nothingness, and the digital nothingness, the realm to which all gods come to die, is entertainment.

Notes

1. Eco, Umberto, *Foucault's Pendulum*. London: Vintage Books, 2001, p. 289.
2. Retrieved from: https://www.nytimes.com/1984/01/01/nyregion/the-message-for-today-in-orwell-s-1984.html.
3. Retrieved from: https://www.openculture.com/2014/01/george-orwell-explains-in-a-revealing-1944-letter-why-hed-write-1984.html.
4. Gruppo di Nun, *Revolutionary Demonology*. Falmouth: Urbanomic Media Ltd, 2022, p. 21.
5. Ibid., p. 17.
6. Ibid., p. 24.
7. Segal, Robert A., *Myth: A Very Short Introduction*. New York: Oxford University Press, 2004., p. 93.
8. Baudrillard, Jean, *Impossible Exchange*, Chris Turner (trans.). London: Verso, 2011, pp. 78–79.

2.

Mirrors and Mirror Apps

> There is a strange affinity between the internet and doomsday. Civilisation's morbid fascination with its own annihilation has often been relegated to the deepest and most anonymous corners of the web, where, next to scam advertisements threatening horrendous bodily deformities, dark omens of death and destruction steal more clicks than even the most depraved pornography. Somehow, secretly, we want to know — in the darkness of our incognito windows — how many seconds, minutes, hours, days, months, and years separate us from our doom. Are we dying of some incurable and disgusting disease? When will the earth be engulfed by the fiery abyss of our expiring sun? A mirror of our most terrifying nightmares is always one Google search away, or even closer, haunting social media with our antisocial urges, as if the Algorithm already knew — and it does — what scares us and excites us the most.
>
> Gruppo di Nun, *Revolutionary Demonology.*[1]

I was a student when I first watched *The Matrix,* like many of the people I knew back then. One distinct change that I noticed around me when the movie came out, besides the sudden growth in the public affinity for black suits, was that people behaved not only as if they had just realized that they live inside a matrix, but as if they were Neo, meaning as if they had just, merely by watching the movie, had overcome the invisible grip of the matrix. To me, this seemed similar to the affinity for zombie apocalypse in movies. People who like this genre may enjoy dressing up as zombies on various occasions, but will imagine themselves not as zombies among the endless hordes of animated, unthinking undead, but as the last human heroes who have endured the apocalypse and are now fighting the zombies. I see two reasons for this. One is the simple inability to think about not thinking, meaning that we cannot conceive what it is like to be a zombie in the same way we cannot conceive what it is like to be dead. In this context, there is an interesting and surprising attempt to illustrate how zombies see the world in the Netflix animated show *Midnight Gospel* (Trussel, 2020). In its first episode, we see that, while zombies do seem monstrous, they perceive the world as a paradise to which they want to invite more and more living creatures.

The second reason why we always imagine ourselves as the free-thinking protagonists is that we want — or we used to want — to be the magicians who act in the world, rather than being a part of everyone and everything else. This is a feature of storytelling and world-building that does not exist in the message of *Black Mirror*.

In the world of *Black Mirror,* virtual simulations are not a form of Gnostic prison, as they used to be in *The Matrix*. Instead, these are either expansions or replacements to the physical world — expansions that, like corrupt magical acts, collapse and fall back on their creators. Through several episodes, *Black Mirror* draws parables to *The Matrix,* in which a man-made, failed attempt at the technological occult leads to the negation of mankind from within. Three important failures are shown in three separate episodes. First, there is a failure in necromancy and the raising of the dead, as shown in the episode "Be Right Back" (Season 02, Episode 01, Harris, 2013). In this episode we are introduced to a technology that can simulate our dead loved ones, first through extrapolation of the digital information that they have spread while alive, through emails, social media, and any other information that can be harvested after their demise. Then, an artificial body of the deceased could be manufactured, into which all relevant information could be downloaded in order to create the perfect clones of the dead. In this episode, however, the protagonist realizes that the clone of her deceased husband, a complex and uncanny monstrosity of a zombie, is not a blessing but a curse that does not grow old, is not human and thus will haunt her until her last day, perhaps before becoming such a zombie herself.

A more dynamic attempt to successfully act in the world is shown in the special episode "White Christmas" (Tibbettes, 2014). In this episode, Matt Trent leads a group of sexual predators who work together in order to successfully seduce women. Morals aside, what Trent does can easily remind us of the operators in *The Matrix*, who sat in the real world and communicated with the heroes who ventured into the simulated matrix, helping them by downloading information into their minds, or giving them information about events unfolding around them. In this man-made, primitive form of a matrix, the virtual and the physical are merged. The eyes of every man and woman are connected (or replaced) with "Z-Eyes," implants that transmit vision and sound both to the brain and online. Through this technology, Trent and his students follow another student, Harry, on his way to find and seduce a random woman in an office Christmas party. He is successful, as Trent is in constant communication with him, delivering him any information he needs in order to converse with and deceive the people in the party to believe he also works for the company, and in order to seduce the woman he chooses. The results are tragic, precisely because the power to talk to an exterior intelligence, the way Harry does, has deep and profound resemblance to conversing with exterior divinities, with demons, with inner mental voices.

In the third failure, the matrix is beginning to be realized. This happens in the episode "Playtest" (Season 03, Episode

02, Trachtenberg, 2016). In this episode, Cooper acts as a test subject and enters the matrix, meaning a virtual world created by a company called SaitoGemu. In this gaming-oriented matrix, both Cooper, the people at the gaming company and the viewers can understand the problems with the uncanny nature of the matrix, as well as the problem with extreme differences between real and virtual time. The realm of the virtual becomes an escape from the material prison of the mundane, physical world — or so it seems in this episode. Within the all-too-real virtual game world, all feelings and uncanny encounters, be they funny or horrific, are entertaining. Cooper's enthusiasm inside the virtual world brings to mind philosopher John Gray's depiction of contemporary cybernauts as Gnostics who attempt to escape the confinements of the physical world. The human body itself seems like nothing but a material prison, while the soul can roam free in a different world where no such restrictions exist.[2] However, that is not the case in Cooper's story, as he dies from a simple malfunction while inside his costume-made matrix, a malfunction caused in the physical world. The wondrous, free world of the virtual is not separated, but firmly attached to the physical world through servers, electricity and electro-magnetic waves. If anything, Cooper's life became much more vulnerable once he thought he existed inside a virtual world.

In *The Matrix*, the matrix is, as mentioned before, merely a Gnostic dream state in which mankind is imprisoned. In *Black Mirror*, however, mankind falls into the trap of believing in the virtual as a universe that can completely replace the physical. This belief is flawed in its entirety not only for the reason presented by Gray, but also (and more importantly) because nothing can be *transferred* into or through the virtual. All we can do is *copy* things. In the same way virtual files are never truly transferred online, but only copied, so the human mind, again — if such feat will ever be possible — will not be transferred into a virtual universe, but merely a virtual copy of it will be created, leaving the original mind – with all its physical burdens – in the material world.

This global mistake is shown in the episode "San Junipero" (Season 03, Episode 04, Harris, 2016). In this episode, a real matrix is created, to which dying people from the physical world can upload their consciousness in order to live forever in a virtual paradise. This paradise is an ongoing, nostalgic reenactment of several decades throughout the twentieth century, thus reaffirming not only that paradise is man-made, but that the very concept of what paradise should be is man-made rather than either divine or natural. This paradise, then, is dead. It is merely an elaborate simulation that is endlessly simulating *itself* for *itself*, as no living being really enjoys it. For us living, the dead in this paradise are still dead, only they are being virtually animated, perhaps able to communicate with us by algorithms extrapolating human behavior and nothing more. "San Junipero" is the corruption of the idea of divine immortality into nostalgic entertainment.

The fantasy of controlling demons leads to the understanding that such control, at best, might be two sided, making the demons control their summoner. The wonders of technology being able to read the will and the orders of the human, lead to the understanding that such technology can also write the will of the human and have the human at its disposal. At a more benign level, stage magicians who pretend to read their audience's minds usually "write" it by forms of suggestion. In this essence, a virtual alternative to this world might end up rewriting the physical world, and if Baudrillard gave as an example Borges' story of the cartographers who replaced their land with the map of their land,[3] a different map altogether can be placed upon the land, or in their mind. This happens in the physical world, as seen in the episode "Men Against Fire" (Season 03, Episode 05, Verbruggen, 2016), in which we see that the technological implants inside the user's eyes and brain do not merely transmit vision and sound but also replace the sensual perceiving of the physical world with an altered, artificial conception of it. Through this manipulation, people that are considered enemies can be perceived as monsters, and poor housing need not be repaired, but merely replaced by a vision of finer habitats. In the episode "Hang the DJ" (Season 04, Episode 04, Van Patten, 2017), the matrix becomes real in the sense that the protagonists of the episode are revealed to be not physical people, but rather their virtual clones.

In the same sense in which Agent Smith is a demon within *The Matrix*, an entity of negation that lacks physical embodiment, the world of *Black Mirror* surfaces a demon in the episode "The Waldo Moment" (Season 02, Episode 03, Higgins, 2013). In this episode, a virtual, fictional character takes over its human host, Jamie Salter, making him behave as it would have behaved. This virtual entity does not merely take over one human, but it is almost elected as prime minister. Waldo is a demon on a personal scale, as much as on a social, national scale. Finally, at the end of the episode, Waldo truly becomes legion, as it spreads in all languages around the world through the many virtual channels, not a matrix per-se, but more of a lymphatic system through which the demon infects the entire human population in the same way any other viral virtuality does.

Finally, *Black Mirror*'s matrix, as it is firmly diffused within the physical world, leads to the redundancy of man, and ultimately to his redundancy and negation in the world. This is shown, as mentioned, in the penetration of technology into the human body, as shown from the episode "The Entire History of You" (Season 01, Episode 03, Welsh, 2011) and onwards. This process transforms the human from an experiencing entity to a recording entity, from a human being to a surveilled, to a surveilling entity. In "White Christmas", and later on in "Black Museum" (Season 04, Episode 06, McCarthy, 2017), the physical human is rendered redundant. In "White Christmas,"

Joe Potter, who is held by the police for murder, is held in his cell while a copy of his mind is being interrogated. Using this method, an interrogation process that takes several virtual years is performed in just a few minutes in the physical world, and a confession that could not have been extracted by the physical suspect is taken from his virtual clone. In "Black Museum," the minds of dead people are transferred not to virtual heaven, but into physical artefacts. In this way, they can be used by their owners even after the death of their physical counterparts, bringing to mind the horror that slaves felt at the thought of becoming zombies after they die, because as zombies they will continue to serve white men even after their death.

Finally, the matrix of *Black Mirror* offers the act of demonization. Back to "White Christmas," Trent is punished for his own crimes by the police, who demonize him through the visual technology of all humanity. He is blocked from society in the physical world, in the same way we block people today on social media. Every visual system in everyone's eyes will now see Trent as a gray, blurry image, and every hearing equipment will transform his talking into an inaudible sound. Trent is demonized not only because he is publicly declared as a villain throughout society, but also because his physicality is taken away from him, and he remains as a ghost wandering around the world, unrecognized as an individual, and unable to recognize others, since these sensory limitations apply to him as well, as to anyone who comes in contact with him. All that remains from him is a virtual, unsettling entity.

In the interactive episode "Bandersnatch," a complete cycle of self-devourment is achieved. As in a computer game, we, the viewers, navigate the protagonist, Stefan Butler, in his determined quest to develop his own video game which offers players a limited number of actions per turn to navigate the hero through the plot. As Butler's game is then described, the limited number of options gives the players the illusion of endless possibilities. This condition is projected, of course, to the interactive episode as well, which merely gives us the illusion of a complex and elaborated story that offers us an endless number of choices to guide Butler through. Exiting "Bandersnatch," I am now sitting in front of the streaming service that seems to offer me an infinite number of shows to choose from, although in the end I do not choose a show I would have otherwise wanted, but rather one that is presented to me by the service (who is servicing who?).

In 2017, an article was published about the CEO of Netflix, Reed Hastings, in which the controversial and rather surprising enemy of the streaming platform was defined. To quote the article:

> More specifically, explains Hastings, there are only a certain amount of hours which humans can tend to activities, and Netflix's goal is to occupy those moments — and deliver the utmost joy to the consumer during that opportunity.
>
> "You get a show or a movie you're really dying to watch, and you end up staying up late at night, so we actually compete with sleep," he said of his No. 1 competitor. Not that he puts too much stock in his rival: "And we're winning!"[4]

One cannot but think about the laboratory rat, endlessly pushing the lever, diminishing in joy into its demise.

Notes

1. Gruppo di Nun, *Revolutionary Demonology*. Falmouth: Urbanomic Media Ltd, 2022, p. 28.
2. For more on Cybernauts and Gnostics, see Gray, John, *Straw Dogs: Thoughts on Humans and Other Animals*. New York: Farrar, Straus and Giroux, 2007, pp. 142–144.

3. Baudrillard, Jean, *Simulacra and Simulation,* Sheila Faria Glaser and Ann Arbor (trans.). The University of Michigan Press, 1994, p. 1.
4. Raphael, Rina, "Netflix CEO Reed Hastings: Sleep Is Our Competition," on *FastCompany*, retrieved from: https://www.fastcompany.com/40491939/netflix-ceo-reed-hastings-sleep-is-our-competition.

3.

Thou Shalt Not

Giovanni Francesco Pico dell Mirandola (the younger) in his *De Praenotione* says that two magicians met in the hall of the queen of England to give an entertainment, having mutually agreed to obey each other implicitly. The first ordered the second to look out of the window; and when he had done so, stag's horns grew from his head, and he was for a long time exposed to the ridicule and jokes of all. So, since he had been powerless under this outrage and wished to avenge himself with a worse one, he drew a human figure with charcoal on the wall, and ordered the first sorcerer to stand under that figure and walk through the wall. The first magician saw instant death in this, and was afraid and began to beg to be excused; but when the other reminded him of their agreement he was compelled to obey, and he was seen to walk through the wall. But he was never found afterwards; for the demon with his higher power had killed him and hidden his body in some deserted place or cave.

Brother Francesco Maria Guazzo, *Compendium Maleficarum*.[1]

In 1973, the artist Chris Burden, aired a ten-second video of his performance, titled *Through the Night Softly* on public television in Los Angeles. In this video, Burden, dressed only in underwear, was crawling across a parking lot filled with broken glass with his hands behind his back, illuminated by a car's headlights. He bought late-night ad time on a local TV station in Los Angeles to broadcast this performance, as he aimed to reach a broad audience and challenge conventional notions of art and media. We can imagine people sitting that night in front of the television screen, watching a series of commercials that promised the good life and a better world through the purchasing and consumption of the products being advertised, only to be interrupted, for ten seconds, by the unsettling and painful video of Burden crawling on broken glass. For a short while, a message disrupted the medium.

Black Mirror premiered with an episode about the ultimate artistic act, much more severe than Burden's performance — the ultimate system crash. In "The National Anthem" (Season 01, Episode 01, Bathurst, 2011), the entire nation comes to a full stop in order to gather around screens and watch the British prime minister as he engages in sexual intercourse with a pig. This act is forced on the prime minister, who is told that, should he refuse to participate in this pornographic live broadcast, a loved princess who was kidnapped will be executed. However, we later learn that the princess, physically unharmed, was released *before* the act took place, and was wandering in the empty streets while everyone was waiting for the promised broadcast. The act was not broadcast for the pleasure of the kidnapper who sent the prime minister and the British audience this threat, as he committed suicide before the act took place, and so did not even watch it. In essence, when this act takes place, everyone watches it while no one truly *wants* it to happen. The princess is already released, the kidnapper is dead and everyone else, while previously enthusiastic about the upcoming grotesque spectacle, is now watching it with horror mixed with disgusted curiosity. Everyone *must* watch it, but no one is forcing them to watch, no one is gaining anything from it, and no one can stop the broadcast. For a while, it is only the live video that exists through the entire British population — millions of helpless hosts taken over by an alien presence — alien both in its content and in its totality.

In this sense, "The National Anthem" is an episode that deals with a demonic spectacle, as this spectacle is founded on demonic rules. Not only must the British Government follow specific rules given by the kidnapper, in order for the princess to be released, but more importantly, the nature of the broadcast that has to be produced manifests a new, unspoken rule. Everyone has to stop everything and watch the disgracing of the prime minister. Through an external event — the kidnapping of the princess, whose pleas for help are broadcasted digitally — the nation undergoes a complete curfew, a temporary and an almost complete shut-down. If in the first *John Wick* movies, the general population was reduced into mindless bystanders by the strict rules of that world, then in this *Black Mirror* episode, the general population is reduced into spectators, forced to watch the unfolding event not because of an external enforcement — as no one is forcing anyone to watch, but simply because they *have* to do so.

A similar incident, at least in the eyes of the character Victoria Skillane, takes place in the *Black Mirror* episode "White Bear" (Season 02, Episode 02, Tibbetts, 2013). In this episode, Skillane awakes in a room, dizzy and unable to remember who she is. When she sees other people through the windows in the buildings around her, they are looking at her and recording her confused attempts to understand what is happening through their phones. As she runs from masked killers, finding another woman who helps her, she understands that the world has gone through something similar to a zombie apocalypse, only digital. It all began when a strange icon appeared on phone screens, turning anyone who saw it, and that means almost everyone, into mindless drones who record everything through their phones. For Skillane, then, the experience is one of being a spectacle that everyone else *has* to record, as they are irrecoverably changed into mindless drones who must comply with this order. Skillane is indeed a spectacle, but in a very different way, as is revealed later in the episode. Nevertheless, like John Wick, she stands against the entire world. In "White Bear," her being and her history become a message of justice, as well (and more importantly) as of entertainment. This message replaces her own internal being, as she is condemned to forget everything she knows with each coming morning. The message of justice destroys the medium that is Victoria Skillane. The message of entertainment destroys the medium that is the notion of justice.

Strict rules, including those who are consensual, are said to separate us from the animals. However, rules that separate humans from the rest of the animals will eventually separate humans from other humans, and humans from their humanity. That is the story that is told in the episode "Nosedive" (Season 03, Episode 01, Wright, 2016). In this episode, a popular application that, we can believe, becomes effectively mandatory within large segments of society, allows people to grade other people and by doing so to increase or decrease their social ranking. Problematic as it is, we can still imagine a benevolent, even if naïve to the point of criminal negligence, use for this application. Through it, one can assume a system that rewards good deeds and punish bad ones. But putting aside the question of who decides what is good and what is bad, we can see in the episode that soon enough, the social system twists around the need to appease the application and to prevent one's grade from diminishing. The grading system, then, shifts from being a system that reacts to human behavior, to a system that rewrites human behavior, promising a severe punishment to those who disobey it, as long as they believe that this punishment is real. Punishment may be society's way to correct those who act against it, but it might erase the humanity out of the one being punished. While this is seen both on "White Bear" and "Nose Dive," perhaps the most extreme seclusion takes place in "White Christmas," as well as in *John Wick*. In both cases, the protagonist is completely banished, or excommunicated, if merely by a procedural law as in *John Wick*, or by completely blocking the punished criminal from the perception of everyone else. Rules can create a conceptual perimeter, outside which humans are no longer considered humans. Rules can lead to a conceptual perimeter within which human behavior is shaped into self-destruction.

Notes

1. Guazzo, Francesco Maria, *Compendium Maleficarum*, E. A. Ashwin (trans.). London: John Rodker, 1929, p. 81.

4.

As Above, So Below

> The act of addressing us is a fundamental aspect of these creatures. The spirits exist only insofar as they speak to us. I believe that the more you read this book, the better you will understand this central and baffling idea. But before we continue, we must ask ourselves a basic question. Why do these spiritual beings have mercy on us in the first place? And why do they choose to speak to us through sudden and striking images? Why is their presence always marked by an odd, eerie, weird apparition? Why do they have to pervert nature in order to reveal their messages? Let us bear in mind that the spirits' alleged warnings never or rarely succeed in modifying the course of history. Notwithstanding the spirits' eloquent presage, Charles VIII did invade and devastate Italy. The spirits' warning, then, wasn't it a useless message? If the spirits had the faculty to foresee the future, why did they bother sending us a message if they knew it would be of no use?
>
> Armando Maggi, *In the Company of Demons*.[1]

There is a symbolic movement of interpretation, if not of direct comparison, between the re-imagining of *The Matrix*, released in 1999, and *Constantine*, released six years later. Judging from a chronological perspective of human culture, religion, and technological changes and complexities, we can say that the West, at least, is more familiar with the religious, even strictly Catholic world of *Constantine* for longer than it is familiar with the technological settings of *The Matrix*. For this reason, when the movie *Constantine* was released, it revealed that the great horror of a simulated human life, as seen in *The Matrix*, is an old story with different settings but with very similar foundations. A very similar move happens in *Black Mirror* as well, with the arrival of demons in its universe.

The first demon to appear in *Black Mirror* reminds us of the Gerasene demon, in that it is not materially present in the world but exists only through the disruption of human self-sovereignty. In the episode "Striking Vipers" (Season 05, Episode 01, Harris, 2019), two friends, Danny Parker and Karl Houghton, meet again at Parker's birthday, after long years without contact. Houghton gives Parker, now a married man, a gift for his birthday — the latest edition of their favorite video game, called "Striking Vipers," in which each player chooses a fighter for a one-on-one combat. Unlike the original game that they used to play in their youth, the latest game takes place in a matrix. In other words, the players' mind is uploaded into the game, allowing them to be fully present in the battle, not by navigating their preferred avatars, but by *being* their chosen characters and by fighting against each other in battles that, while unharmful, seem very real. The two friends choose their preferred martial arts characters — a male fighter for Parker and a female fighter for Houghton. Then, something unexpected happens. The violent battle quickly changes into a sensual lovemaking, which at first terrifies the two friends, and later tempts them to go back to the simulated world and have virtual sex with each other. Parker is cheating on his wife with his friend Houghton-as-a-woman, and Houghton prefers having sex with Parker's male virtual character over his many female sexual encounters in the physical world. Believing that they might be physically attracted to each other in the physical world as well, and that this suppressed sexual attraction takes place in the secret, free world of the virtual, Parker tries to kiss Houghton in a dark street alley in the physical world. Understanding that this is not the case, they realize that their wild sexual attraction to each other takes place only in the other world, only as the two specific characters they prefer to play as.

At first, this incident brings to mind other incidents that might look similar, in which a game that was intended to be violent becomes as sexual as it is violent. This happens, for instance, in the world of the TV series *Westworld* (Nolan, Joy, 2016) in a technological theme park that resembles the wild west. In this story, the theme park, a huge, technologically advanced expanse that is populated with lifelike androids that offer the visitors stories, missions, and the seemingly real immersion in the fantasy of the wild west, quickly becomes a place for rich visitors to come in order to rape and murder androids without facing any moral consequences. Indeed, each android, so lifelike that it really thinks it is a human being, is repaired and forgets about its miserable past with each morning. The difference, however, is important. In the *Black Mirror* episode, the two friends do not want, at first, to turn the game into a sexual platform, and are in fact horrified by how the game is changing them.

This demon, the game, is not exorcised in the story of Parker and Houghton. In fact, it alters their lives and resides in their minds from the moment they turn on the game. Why does this demon do what it does? The episode offers no apparent reason. We can say that this demon acts in the world through the anti-human manipulation of the will, haunting these two friends and acting solely to sustain and amplify its own presence by doing so.

A very different demon, more comical and much more violent, appears in the episode "Demon 79" (Season 06, Episode 05, Haynes, 2023). This episode takes place in England in 1979, and unlike the vast majority of the *Black Mirror* episodes, which take place in the near future, or even in an alternate, technological past, like the episode "Beyond the Sea" (Season 06, Episode 03, Crowley, 2023) which takes place in an alternate 1969, "Demon 79" lacks any depiction of technological advancement or even a technological discourse. Its story revolves around pre-election Britain and the possible rise of a prime minister from a far-right political party. The protagonist of the episode is an Indian girl, Nida Huq, who is working as a shoe saleswoman in a big department store. While constantly harassed by her xenophobic peers and customers, Huq is forced to eat her traditional Biryani in the basement. There, in the forgotten bowels of the department store, she comes across old newspaper articles and a strange talisman. Holding it, she accidentally pricks her finger, summoning a demon called Gaap by doing so. If, so far, *Black Mirror* offered a discourse about the subnatural demonic through technology and its effects on humans, this final episode of the sixth season offers, instead, a real, supernatural demon. If the rest of the series was comparable to *The Matrix*, this episode is *Black Mirror*'s *Constantine*.

The demon Gaap (or Tap, as described in the *Dictionnaire Infernal*),[2] is described in grimoires such as the *Lesser Key of Solomon* as the thirty-third spirit, who is a great president and a mighty prince. He appears in human shape before great kings, as a guide to offer them help along their way, teaching philosophy and liberal sciences. Gaap causes intense emotions like love or hatred, as well as rendering men insensible.[3] In the *Black Mirror* episode, Gaap appears to Huq, first as a monstrous demon, displaying every familiar demonic characteristic — red skin, cloven hoofs, black horns etc. But when he realizes Huq is terrified by his appearance, he chooses a different, more friendly form — that of Boney M's singer, Bobby Farrell. Doing his best to calm Huq and being as friendly as possible, Gaap does deliver terrible news. Since she summoned him, she is required to murder three people in the next few days. Failing to do so will not only result in Gaap's eternal banishment into the void but will also bring about the end of the world for mankind. Gaap, being visible only to Huq, tries to convince her to do as expected of her, selecting victims for her whom he claims deserve to die. Huq does not want to commit these acts of murder but is quickly drawn into committing a series of murders. Is she dreaming or is she indeed haunted by a demon that tries to help her prevent the end of the world? Huq finds out that everything — the murders, the demon and the end of the world — are all very real.

"Demon 79" seems detached from the rest of the *Black Mirror* Universe, and was even released as a *Red Mirror* production, promising horror stories instead of dystopian speculative narratives about the near future. However, two visual aspects in the episode do indeed connect the supernatural story of Gaap's appearance on Earth and the subnatural and demonic presence of technology in the world. The first aspect is the symbol that is first shown in the episode "White Bear," appearing on the magical item that summons Gaap, as well as in other places throughout the episode. The second aspect is the ghostly glow in Huq's eyes, as Gaap makes her see visions. This glow seems identical to the glow in the eyes of people who use the Z-Eyes technology throughout the numerous *Black Mirror* episodes. This reappearance of effects that correspond first to technology and then to demonology can be understood simply as the visual characteristics that represent the universe of *Black Mirror*. However, they may also hint at a connection between the two, seemingly distant worlds of technology and demonology. Indeed, judging from the chronology of human culture, as it is presented in *Black Mirror*, rather than the chronology of the episodes themselves, we can see that the same symbols and effects on the human, symbols and effects that were once attributed to demonology, resurface again in a world in which demonology is seemingly extinct, and technology reigns. If this is true, then the technology shown in the *Black Mirror* universe is merely a new method of channeling old demonic messages into the human medium, before it becomes a tool for mankind. In an age when widespread magic is dead, the demonic will find a new way to emerge.

The reappearance of the supernatural horror in a new, updated, seemingly disenchanted emergence of the subnatural is at the very core of *Black Mirror*. This blackened mirror, meaning the turned-off black screens that are everywhere around us, on mobile phones and television screens, has an origin that begins in a very different world in which technology was magical. The first black mirror to be used in the West was probably the black mirror that was used in the sixteenth century by John Dee, an astronomer, occultist and alchemist, together with his partner, the occultist Edward Kelley, as an advisor to Queen Elizabeth I.[4] Dee and Kelley were engaged in attempts to contact angels and spirits in rituals for what they believed would greatly help mankind. As a tool for this act of summoning, the two used a black, obsidian mirror that was brought from Mexico and created by the Aztecs. This black mirror, an artefact from the past which was used by Dee and Kelley in order to contact virtual spirits, returns centuries later in mass produced form in order to make billions of people see similar virtual visions.

Technology changes. Magic remains. Words change. The spiritual and the demonic are now virtual. Are we possessed into being convinced that we are no longer possessed?

Notes

1. Maggi, Armando, *In the Company of Demons: Unnatural Beings, Love, and Identity in the Italian Renaissance*. Chicago: University of Chicago Press, 2008, p. viii.
2. De Plancy, Jacques Collin, *Dictionnaire Infernal*. Paris: Henry Plon, Imprimeur-Éditeur, 1863, p. 651.

3. Peterson, Joseph H. (ed.), *The Lesser Key of Solomon (Legemeton Clavicula Salomonis): Detailing the Ceremonial Art of Commanding Spirits both Good and Evil*. York Beach: Weiser Books, 2001, p. 22.
4. More about John Dee can be found here: Louv, Jason, *John Dee and the Empire of Angels: Enochian Magick and the Occult Roots of the Modern World*. Rochester: Inner Traditions, 2018.

Archangel Michael Slays the Dragon

Time is not important, only life is important.
The Fifth Element, Luc Besson, 1997.

If reality is a simulation, then for us it is a simulation without the original and prime source that is simulated. It is either a simulation created by a god or by other sentient beings. If it is not a simulation, then it instantly copies itself into a simulation in our minds, when we attempt to reduce it from the chaotic combination of the anti-human, the non-human and the human to a humanistic translation of it. In either case, whether by bug or by feature, our self-sovereignty, if it ever existed in the first place, is negated by external beings, meontological in their essence, regardless of any mythological approach to their existence. These negating beings, demons, can be regarded as the same non-personal beings that were once widely conceived as supernatural, and may now be regarded as subnatural, emerging not from a transcendent realm, but from the technological creations of mankind.

Contemporary demonology revolves not around the satanic essence of old mythologies about demons and their affairs in the human world, but around the demonic entropy, growing ever stronger and ever pulling us towards its event horizon, toward oblivion. Everything weakens. Everything dies. The human can only have so much understanding of the non-human. But mankind can indeed battle with the demons of entropy by accepting the importance of the non-human vibrancy. Unlike past battles with the demonic, which were not only humanistic in their essence, but indeed saw the demon in the eyes of the non-human beast, this book suggests a different method to defeat entropy, not by detaching mankind from the world, but by reconnecting it.

Coming back to Descartes' demon, we might not be able to discern what he might have called an authentic thought and the thought that is infecting us by an external message, compromising us as its medium in the process. Unable to rely on the independence of our own internal core, we can — by understanding the concept of the demon — act in ways that can subvert its method of negation. To oppose entropy, one must promote life. Throughout human history, death is promoted far more than life is. Death is promoted by a mythology that favors the dedication of earthly life to the aftermath that follows the physical death, or by politics and economy, in which suffering and death of others (and even one's own death!) are justified as a means to an end. From a non-human perspective, humanity's presence on Earth is an unrivaled catalyst for the staggering number of non-human animal deaths. Death and non-sentience (this separates dangerous germs and viruses from other beings) are the great attractors that leads life, to the point where we might find it more practical and logical to search for intelligent life on other worlds not by their own presence, but by the presence of the after-life — technological debris that might remain after their exctinction.[1]

On a long enough timeline, we cannot conceive entropy as beatable in any way. The sun will swallow the earth, and the universe will die a cold death. But on more local perspective, a shift from the promotion of death to the promotion of sentient life — not of my own life, not of mankind's life, but of sentient life in itself — may be the key to defeat such demons of entropy. The appreciation of life, that of people of other cultures, that of non-humans that are today being lined up and executed in order to become food for humans, can lead to the refusal to dominate and manipulate others. Such refusal can then lead to the conceiving of technology that will not be considered neutral or harmful, but rather benevolent. To my understanding, this may be the key to resisting – if not defeating - what Lovecraft calls "Cosmic Horror" and what Mark Fisher calls "Capital Realism,"[2] both discussing the hopelessness of mankind in front of a vast anti-human monstrosity that is uncaring of its own interests and will for sovereignty. Life, in its essence, is resistance to entropy. Life, on a more mythological level of conceptualization, might be the very excess that can ultimately break this simulation of descent into nihil.

Notes

1. Loeb, Avi, *Extraterrestrial: The First Sign of Intelligent Life Beyond*, Idit Shorer (trans.). Hevel Modi'in: Kinneret, Zmora, Dvir, 2021.
2. Fisher, Mark, *Capitalist Realism: Is There No Alternative?* London: John Hunt Publishing, 2009.

Bibliography

Afanasyv, Alexander, *Russian Folk Tale: A Dual Language Book*, Sergey Levchin (trans.). Mineola: Dover Publishing, 2014.

Agamben, Giorgio, *The Mystery of Evil: Benedict XVI and the End of Days*, Adam Kotsko (trans.). Stanford: Stanford University Press, 2017.

Baudrillard, Jean, *Simulacra and Simulation*, Sheila Faria Glaser and Ann Arbor (trans.). The University of Michigan Press, 1994.

Baudrillard, Jean, *Impossible Exchange*, Chris Turner (trans.). London: Verso, 2011.

Blish, James, *The Devil's Day*. New York: Baen Publishing Enterprises, 1971.

Borges, Jorge Luis, *Collected Fictions*, Andrew Hurley (trans.). London: Penguin books, 1999.

Bruno, Giordano, *Cause, Principle and Unity: And Essays on Magic*, Richard J. Blackwell (trans.). Robert de Luca, Cambridge: Cambridge University Press, 2004.

Burckhardt, Titus, *Alchemy: Science of the Cosmos, Science of the Soul*, William Stoddart (trans.). Baltimore: Penguin Books, 1972.

Dante, Alighieri, Amari-Parker, Anna (ed.), *Dante's Divine Comedy: Hell, Purgatory, Paradise*, Henry W. Longfellow (trans.). London: Arcturus Publishing Limited, 2006.

Davis, Owen, *Grimoires: A History of Magic Books*. Oxford: Oxford University Press, 2009.

De Plancy, Jacques Collin, *Dictionnaire Infernal*. Paris: Henry Plon, Imprimeur-Éditeur, 1863.

Deudney, Daniel, *Dark Skies: Space Expansionism, Planetary Geopolitics & the Ends of Humanity*. New York: Oxford University Press, 2020.

Eco, Umberto, *Foucault's Pendulum*. London: Vintage Books, 2001.

Fisher, Mark, *Capitalist Realism: Is There No Alternative?* London: John Hunt Publishing, 2009.

Gaiman, Neil, *The Books of Magic*. New York: DC Comics, 2001.

Gray, John, *Straw Dogs: Thoughts on Humans and Other Animals*. New York: Farrar, Straus and Giroux, 2007.

Gray John, *Black Mass: How Religion Led the World into Crisis*. London: Penguin Books, 2008.

Gruppo di Nun, *Revolutionary Demonology*. Falmouth: Urbanomic Media Ltd, 2022.

Guazzo, Francesco Maria, *Compendium Maleficarum*, E. A. Ashwin (trans.). London: John Rodker, 1929.

Harraway, Donna J., *Staying with the Trouble: Making Kin in the Chthulucene*. Durham: Duke University Press, 2016.

Jonas, Hans, *The Gnostic Religion: The Message of the Alien God and the Beginning of Christianity*. Boston: Beacon Press, 1991.

Land, Nick, *The Thirst for Annihilation: Georges Bataille and Virulent Nihilism (an Essay in Atheistic Religion)*. London: Routledge, 1992.

Lecouteux, Claude, *The Book of Grimoires: The Secret Grammar of Magic*, Jon E. Graham (trans.). Rochester: Inner Traditions, 2013.

Lévi, Éliphas, *Transcendental Magic: Its Doctrine and Ritual*, Arthur Edward Waite (trans.). Mansfield Centre: Martino Publishing, 2011.

Loeb, Avi, *Extraterrestrial: The First Sign of Intelligent Life Beyond*, Idit Shorer (trans.). Hevel Modi'in: Kinneret, Zmora, Dvir, 2021.

Louv, Jason, *John Dee and the Empire of Angels: Enochian Magick and the Occult Roots of the Modern World*. Rochester: Inner Traditions, 2018.

Lovecraft, H. P., *The Call of Cthulhu and Other Weird Stories*, S. T. Joshi (ed.). London: Penguin Books, 2002.

MacCormack, Patricia, *The Ahuman Manifesto: Activism for the End of the Anthropocene*. London: Bloomsbury Academic, 2020.

Maggi, Armando, *In the Company of Demons: Unnatural Beings, Love, and Identity in the Italian Renaissance*. Chicago: University of Chicago Press, 2008.

Marlowe, Christopher, *Doctor Faustus*, John D. Jump (ed.). London: Routledge, 2005.

Moore, Alan and Gibbons, Dave, *Watchmen*. New York: DC Comics, 1987.

Nagel, Thomas, "What Is It Like to Be a Bat?" in *The Philosophical Review*, Vol. 83, No. 4 (October 1974), Duke University Press, pp. 435–450.

Pascal, Blaise, *Pensées and Other Writings*, Honor Levi (trans.). Oxford: Oxford University Press, 1999.

Peterson, Joseph H. (ed.), *The Lesser Key of Solomon (Legemeton Clavicula Salomonis): Detailing the Ceremonial Art of Commanding Spirits Both Good and Evil*. York Beach: Weiser Books, 2001.

Segal, Robert A., *Myth: A Very Short Introduction*. New York: Oxford University Press, 2004.

Serres, Michel, *The Parasite*. Lawrence R. Schehr (trans). Minneapolis: University of Minneapolis Press, 2007.

Shelley, Percy Bysshe, *Prometheus Unbound, A Lyrical Drama*. Boston: D. C. Heath & Co., 1892.

Skinner, B. F., *Beyond Freedom and Dignity*. Harmondsworth: Penguin Books, 1976.

Strachey, James (ed.), *The Standard Edition of the Complete Psychological Works of Sigmund Freud*, James Stachey (trans). London: The Hogarth Press, 1981.

Strickland, Lloyd and Lewis, Harry, *Leibniz on Binary: The Invention of Computer Arithmetic*. Cambridge: MIT Press, 2022.

Swetz, Frank, J., "Leibniz, the Yijing, and the Religious Conversion of the Chinese," in *Mathematics Magazine*, 2003, 76:4, pp. 276–291.

Thacker, Eugene, *Cosmic Pessimism*. Minneapolis: Univocal Publishing, 2015.

Thacker, Eugene, *In the Dust of this Planet: Horror of Philosophy*, Vol. 1. Winchester: Zero Books, 2011.

Thacker, Eugene, *Starry Speculative Corpse: Horror of Philosophy*, Vol. 2. Winchester: Zero Books, 2015.

Tyson, Donald, *The Demonology of King James I*. Woodbury: Llewellyn Publications, 2011.

Zakai, Avihu, *The Disenchantment of the World: Science and Religion in the Early Modern Period*. Tel Aviv: Resling, 2018.

Zizék, Slavoj, *Trouble in Paradise: From the End of History to the End of Capitalism*. UK: Penguin Books, 2015.

Zizék, Slavoj, *Violence: Six Sideways Reflections*. New York: Picador, 2008.

Zuboff, Shoshana, *The Age of Surveillance Capitalism: The Fight for a Human Future at the New Frontier of Power*. New York: Public Affairs, 2019.

6TH
BOOKS

ALL THINGS PARANORMAL

Investigations, explanations and deliberations on the paranormal, supernatural, explainable or unexplainable. 6th Books seeks to give answers while nourishing the soul: whether making use of the scientific model or anecdotal and fun, but always beautifully written.
Titles cover everything within parapsychology: how to, lifestyles, alternative medicine, beliefs, myths and theories.
If you have enjoyed this book, why not tell other readers by posting a review on your preferred book site?

Recent Bestsellers from 6th Books Are:

The Scars of Eden

Paul Wallis

How do we distinguish between our ancestors' ideas of God and close encounters of an extraterrestrial kind?

Paperback: 978-1-78904-852-0 ebook: 978-1-78904-853-7

The Afterlife Unveiled

Stafford Betty

What the dead are telling us about their world! What happens after we die? Spirits speaking through mediums know, and they want us to know. This book unveils their world...

Paperback: 978-1-84694-496-3 ebook: 978-1-84694-926-5

Harvest: The True Story of Alien Abduction

G.L. Davies

G.L. Davies's most-terrifying investigation yet reveals one woman's terrifying ordeal of alien visitation, nightmarish visions and a prophecy of destruction on a scale never before seen in Pembrokeshire's peaceful history.

Paperback: 978-1-78904-385-3 ebook: 978-1-78904-386-0

M.E. Myself and I: Diary of a Psychic

Nicky Alan

A brutally honest journey showing strength of the human spirit, faith in the unseen and a tenacious will to survive.

Paperback: 978-1-78904-451-5 ebook: 978-1-78904-452-2

Phantoms of Christmas Past

Paul Weatherhead

True stories of seasonal ghost hoaxes and strange phantom panics from the nineteenth and early twentieth centuries.

Paperback: 978-1-80341-840-7 ebook: 978-1-80341-866-7

Spirit Release

Sue Allen

A guide to psychic attack, curses, witchcraft, spirit attachment, possession, soul retrieval, haunting, deliverance, exorcism and more, as taught at the College of Psychic Studies.

Paperback: 978-1-84694-033-0 ebook: 978-1-84694-651-6

Advanced Psychic Development

Becky Walsh

Learn how to practise as a professional, contemporary spiritual medium.

Paperback: 978-1-84694-062-0 ebook: 978-1-78099-941-8

Where After

Mariel Forde Clarke

A journey that will compel readers to view life after death in a completely different way.

Paperback: 978-1-78904-617-5 ebook: 978-1-78904-618-2

Paranormal Perspectives: One Big Box of 'Paranormal Tricks'?

John Fraser

Think Zen and the Art of Spending the Night in a Haunted House, a celebration of the dream of finding something undiscovered and different.

Paperback: 978-1-80341-524-6 ebook: 978-1-80341-532-1

Haunted: Horror of Haverfordwest

G.L. Davies

Blissful beginnings for a young couple turn into a nightmare after purchasing their dream home in Wales in 1989.

Paperback: 978-1-78535-843-2 ebook: 978-1-78535-844-9

Astral Projection Made Easy and overcoming the fear of death

Stephanie June Sorrell

From the popular Made Easy series, Astral Projection Made Easy helps to eliminate the fear of death through discussion of life beyond the physical body.

Paperback: 978-1-84694-611-0 ebook: 978-1-78099-225-9

Developing Your Supernatural Awareness

Fredrick Woodard

The common themes and details pointed out in this book will develop or enhance your understanding of our supernatural awareness and connection with our interactive universe.

Paperback: 978-1-80341-478-2 ebook: 978-1-80341-479-9

Readers of ebooks can buy or view any of these bestsellers by clicking on the live link in the title. Most titles are published in paperback and as an ebook. Paperbacks are available in traditional bookshops. Both print and ebook formats are available online.

Find more titles and sign up to our readers' newsletter at **www.6th-books.com**

Join the 6th books Facebook group at **6th Books The world of the Paranormal**